# SURRENDER
## AT
# NEW ORLEANS

D1041805

**David Rooney** served in the Queen's Royal Regiment in India and West Africa at the end of the Second World War. After leaving the Army he read history at Oxford, and his career in education took him to Ulster, Germany and the Royal Military Academy Sandhurst as a Senior Lecturer. His published works include *Burma Victory*, *Wingate and the Chindits*, *Military Mavericks*, *Guerrilla* and *Mad Mike*, the biography of the late Brigadier Michael Calvert DSO, which is in print with Pen & Sword.

**Michael Scott** was commissioned into the Scots Guards in 1960. After worldwide regimental service, he commanded 2nd Battalion Scots Guards in the Falklands War and was awarded the DSO. He subsequently commanded a brigade in Northern Ireland and, as a Major General, became GOC Scotland and Governor of Edinburgh Castle in 1993. On leaving the Army, he was appointed Complaints Commissioner to the Bar Council. His great-great-grandfather, Captain Archie Stewart, fought throughout the Peninsula Campaign and at Waterloo in Harry Smith's Rifle Brigade. His second book *Scapegoats – Thirteen Victims of Military Injustice* was published in March 2013.

# SURRENDER
## AT
# NEW ORLEANS

## GENERAL SIR HARRY SMITH
### IN THE PENINSULA AND AMERICA

### DAVID ROONEY & MICHAEL SCOTT

Pen & Sword
**MILITARY**

First published in Great Britain in 2008 as In Love and War
and reprinted in this format in 2014 by
PEN & SWORD MILITARY
An imprint of
Pen & Sword Books Ltd
47 Church Street
Barnsley, South Yorkshire
S70 2AS

ISBN 978 1 78383 120 3

A CIP catalogue record for this book is
available from the British Library

Typeset in 11pt Ehrhardt by
Sylvia Menzies-Earl, Pen & Sword Books Ltd

Printed and bound in England
By CPI Group (UK) Ltd, Croydon, CR0 4YY

Pen & Sword Books Ltd incorporates the Imprints of Aviation, Atlas,
Family History, Fiction, Maritime, Military, Discovery, Politics, History,
Archaeology, Select, Wharncliffe Local History, Wharncliffe True Crime,
Military Classics, Wharncliffe Transport, Leo Cooper, The Praetorian Press,
Remember When, Seaforth Publishing and Frontline Publishing

For a complete list of Pen & Sword titles please contact
PEN & SWORD BOOKS LIMITED
47 Church Street, Barnsley, South Yorkshire, S70 2AS, England
E-mail: enquiries@pen-and-sword.co.uk
Website: www.pen-and-sword.co.uk

# Contents

# List of Maps

# Acknowledgements

In writing this book, we have not attempted to indulge in a detailed military history of the times but rather to use that history as a backcloth to the love story of Harry and Juana. Purists might therefore blame us for skating over the detail, say, of Waterloo or many of the Peninsula War battles. While these were, of course, important we have only been more specific in the battles vital to the story, such as Badajoz and Aliwal. We have tried to use primary sources, where possible, at the National Archives at Kew, the National Army Museum and, of course, Christopher Robinson's memorabilia, but have, with gratitude, leant on many of the outstanding books listed in the Bibliography.

We must thank Charles Messenger for suggesting our meeting and his support and guidance with the project.

The Museums at Whittlesey and the Rifles at Winchester have been invaluable – we could not have done this without Maureen Watson at the former and Ken Gray at the latter. We are indebted to the Trustees of the Rifles Museum for permission to publish Harry's portrait and to Maureen for the various photographs and documents from Whittlesey. We also thank Geoff Oldfield and his wife, Margaret, for allowing us into St Mary's Church and directing us to Harry and Juana's grave. The Curator of the Queen's Royal Lancers Museum, Captain Holtby, and David Nalson helped us with the exploits of the outstanding 16th Lancers at Aliwal. Photographs have all been taken by Louisa Scott (www.louisascottphotography.com), except where differently noted. Maps are sketched from those in Fortescue's History of the British Army published in 1920, with the exception of Aliwal which hangs on the wall of the new 'Hero of Aliwal' pub in Whittlesey. The landlady was tickled with the idea of our book and gladly gave us permission to publish it!

Christopher Robinson, Harry's great-great-nephew, was exceptionally helpful in allowing us complete access to all his papers, plus Harry's and Juana's medals, portraits and busts. This was the golden nugget of our research and we are eternally grateful to him for permission to use as much as we wanted in the book.

Finally, as the artist relies on the gallery owner, we could not have done this without the help and encouragement of Kathy Rooney, our agent, Henry Wilson, our publisher, and Keyth Rooney and Jim Gracey for technical advice, to whom we owe much thanks.

David Rooney and Michael Scott
Cambridge and London

# Chronology

| | | |
|---|---|---|
| 1787 | 28 June | Harry born in Whittlesey |
| 1798 | 27 March | Juana born in Spain |
| 1805 | 8 May | Harry commissioned |
| 1806-7 | | Monte Video and Buenos Aires expedition |
| 1808-9 | | With Sir John Moore at the Battle of Corunna |
| 1809 | 25 May | Return to the Peninsula under Sir Arthur Wellesley |
| | 28 July | Talavera |
| 1810 | 24 July | Battle of the Coa (wounded) |
| 1811 | 5 May | Fuentes d'Onoro |
| 1812 | 19 January | Storming of Ciudad Rodrigo |
| | 6 April | Storming of Badajoz |
| | 20 April | Harry and Juana married |
| | 22 July | Battle of Salamanca |
| | August | Occupation of Madrid |
| | November | Retreat to the lines of Torres Vedras |
| 1813 | 21 June | Battle of Vitoria |
| | July | Advance to Vera |
| | 27/28 July | The Pyrenees |
| | 31 August | The two battles of Vera. Death of Cadoux. |
| | 10 November | Battle of Nivelle |
| | 12 December | Harry's mother dies |
| 1814 | 27 February | Battle of Orthez |
| | 20 March | Battle of Tarbes |
| | 10 April | Battle of Toulouse |
| | | End of the war |
| | | Harry parts from Juana before starting for the war in America |
| | August | Battle of Bladensburg, capture of Washington, White House burnt |
| | 30 August | Harry sent home with dispatches |
| | December | Harry receives orders to return to America under Sir Edward Pakenham |

|        |              |                                                                      |
|--------|--------------|----------------------------------------------------------------------|
|        | 24 December  | Treaty of Ghent signed                                               |
| 1815   | 8 January    | Battle of New Orleans                                                |
|        | 18 January   | British forces withdraw                                             |
|        | 11 February  | Capture of Fort Bowyer                                              |
|        |              | Ile Dauphine                                                         |
|        | 14 February  | End of the American War (news of Treaty of Ghent reaches America)   |
|        |              | Harry returns to England                                            |
|        |              | Napoleon returns to power                                           |
|        | 18 June      | Battle of Waterloo                                                  |
|        |              | Harry Quartermaster General of the Reserve                         |
|        |              | Promoted Lieutenant Colonel. Awarded CB.                           |
| 1816   | January      | 6th Division moved from Neuilly to St Germain                       |
|        |              | 6th Division reduced. Harry rejoins Regiment as captain.            |
|        |              | Appointed Town Major of Cambrai                                    |
| 1816-18|              | Cambrai                                                              |
| 1818   | 31 October   | Return to England                                                   |
|        | December     | Harry rejoins Regiment at Shorncliffe and Gosport                   |
| 1819-25|              | Glasgow                                                              |
|        |              | Harry Brigade Major during radical disturbances                    |
| 1825   |              | Harry rejoins Regiment in Ireland                                   |
|        | 30 July      | To Nova Scotia                                                       |
|        | 23 November  | Harry leaves his old Regiment and is appointed Deputy Quartermaster General in Jamaica. |
|        |              | Epidemic of yellow fever                                            |
| 1828   | 24 July      | Appointed Deputy Quartermaster General at the Cape of Good Hope     |
| 1829   |              | Harry and Juana travel to South Africa via England                 |
| 1834   |              | First Kaffir War                                                    |
| 1837   | 17 September | Peace                                                                |
| 1840   | 4 June       | Harry and Juana leave Cape Town for India                          |

|       |              | Harry appointed Adjutant General of the Army in India |
|-------|--------------|-------------------------------------------------------|
|       |              | First Afghan War |
| 1843  | 29 December  | Battle of Maharajpore |
|       |              | Harry appointed KCB |
| 1845  |              | Outbreak of the First Sikh War |
|       | 18 December  | Battle of Moodkee |
|       | 21 December  | Battle of Ferozeshah |
| 1846  | 28 January   | Battle of Aliwal |
|       |              | Battle of Sobraon |
|       | 4 April      | Made baronet and raised to GCB |
| 1847  | 29 April     | Return to England |
|       | 24 September | Appointed Governor of the Cape of Good Hope and leaves for South Africa |
|       | 1 December   | Harry and Juana arrive South Africa |
| 1848  | 3 February   | Proclamation of the Orange River Sovereignty |
|       |              | Disaffection among the Boers in the Sovereignty |
|       | 29 August    | Battle of Boomplatz |
| 1849–50 |            | Convict question |
| 1850  | September    | Kaffir war resumes |
| 1852  | 24 January   | Grey's dispatch recalling Harry |
|       | 17 April     | Harry and Juana leave for England |
|       | 1 June       | Arrive Portsmouth |
| 1853  | 21 January   | District Commander |
| 1860  | 12 October   | Harry dies |
| 1872  | 10 October   | Juana dies |

# Introduction to 2014 Edition

Five years ago, *In Love and War* was published. The book told the story of the extraordinary lives of Sir Harry and Lady Smith and their abiding love, which sustained them through so many adventures.

It seems fitting, to mark the 200th anniversary of the momentous year of 1814, which saw the end of the war between Britain and America, that the book should be brought out again in this new format. The battle of New Orleans, although taking place in early 1815 because the news of the Treaty of Ghent had not been received, was the most significant American success of the war. For Harry, ever the professional soldier, this was the nadir of his achievement to date but, nevertheless, it was his advice to General Lambert to call it a day which, ultimately, saved many lives on both sides. Harry himself conveyed the British surrender terms to General Jackson who received him with utmost civility.

Although Harry returned to Juana in the deepest gloom, their lives were to be crowned with many successes at Waterloo, South Africa and India, gaining the admiration of both Wellington and Queen Victoria.

# Chapter 1

# Badajoz
# April 1812

O n 7 April 1812, Badajoz, the proud and elegant Spanish city, which dominated the route from southern Portugal into Spain, lay in smoking ruins. Wellington's army had besieged the town for three weeks and during the final assault which started at 10.00pm the previous evening, they had lost over 2,000 men killed and wounded. At that time, when a city was besieged, it was the convention that on its capture, the attacking troops were given a free hand. The infuriated British soldiers, who had suffered weeks of privation and hardship in the siege and who had seen hundreds of their comrades killed in the attack, went berserk. Wellington himself could not stop them. Although he erected a gallows in the town, not a man was hanged. This is astonishing given Wellington's reputation as a hard disciplinarian. Maybe it was that he understood so well what his men had been through. Indeed, he wrote, 'The storming of Badajoz affords as strong an instance of the gallantry of our troops as has ever been displayed. But I greatly hope that I shall never again be the instrument of putting them to such a test as that to which they were put last night.'

Among Wellington's staff were a number of articulate and literate men, and the capture of Badajoz – the greatest atrocity committed by the British Army since the massacres of Drogheda and Wexford in 1649 – is well documented. Two young captains, Johnny Kincaid and Harry Smith, hardened veterans of Britain's Peninsula battles, who had led their men in the attack, and whose uniforms were torn by musket balls, both described the ghastly scenes.

Later, Captain Smith, wrote in his autobiography: 'It was appalling. Heaps on heaps of slain – in one spot lay nine officers.' Smith continued:

> Now comes a scene of horror I would willingly bury in oblivion. The atrocities committed by our soldiers on the poor innocent and defenceless inhabitants of the city no words suffice to depict. Civilised man, when let loose and the bonds of morality relaxed, is a far greater beast than the savage, more refined in his cruelty, more fiend-like in his every act.

As the marauding troops spread through the town, they ransacked every house, they desecrated every church and cathedral, and from the convents they dragged the nuns by their habits and raped them. Every store of liquor was quickly smashed, and then every man, woman and child became victims of wild drunken excess. Drink-crazed men staggered along clutching priceless artefacts, until a stronger man seized them or until they all collapsed in a drunken stupor. Through the day and into the night, smoke and flames added a lurid glow to the scenes of devastation.

Johnny Kincaid in *Adventures in the Rifle Brigade*, published in 1830, described in great detail how he was standing outside their tents with his friend Harry Smith, observing with horror the mayhem and the drunken debauchery, when two Spanish ladies approached them and begged for protection. The older woman explained in a confident and haughty manner that they belonged to an old and honourable Spanish family, and, after the Battle of Talavera in 1809, a senior British officer, Lord Fitzroy Somerset, had lived in their house, which had now been burnt and destroyed by marauding bands of drunken soldiers. As she spoke, blood was running down the necks of this woman and her younger sister, because soldiers had torn out their earrings. Some officers had lost their lives that day in trying to protect Spanish women from drunken attack, but this encounter was to have a happier outcome.

Kincaid then described the woman's younger sister, Juana, who was in a state of collapse. He wrote: 'A being more transcendingly lovely I had never before seen ... her face was so irresistibly attractive, surmounting a figure cast in nature's fairest mould, that to look at her was to love her. I did love her, but never told my love, and in the meantime another and more impudent fellow stepped in and won her.' The impudent fellow was his fellow officer and lifelong friend Harry Smith.

Harry was twenty-four, Juana fourteen. He was known throughout Wellington's army as the most impetuous, eager and energetic officer, always anxious to shine whether in riding, hunting or leading from the front in battle. He also spoke fluent Spanish. When he first even mentioned the idea of marrying Juana, all his friends were absolutely aghast. Harry, considered by all to have an outstanding and successful career ahead of him, was warned not to throw away such dazzling prospects. How could marriage possibly succeed when he was out campaigning for days at a time, when he was always in the thick of the fighting and when the living conditions even for officers were appalling? He was reminded that he was a staunch Protestant and she was a devout Roman Catholic, who had only recently emerged from the stultifying regime of a Spanish convent. How could such a sheltered young girl adapt to the rigours and hardships of campaigning life when, in Wellington's phrase, she would be surrounded night and day by the scum of the earth?

Harry replied to his critics that he would be a better officer because he would be inspired by her love, and she would understand that all his efforts would be for her. He added, 'Although both of us were of the quickest tempers, we were both ready to forgive, and both intoxicated in happiness.'

Having brushed aside the warnings of his friends, Harry obtained Wellington's permission to marry, and the Duke, renowned for his disapproval of having women in his headquarters, even agreed to give away the bride. A drumhead service was quickly arranged, and on 20 April the Roman Catholic chaplain of the 88th (later the Connaught Rangers) married the pair. There was no time for even the briefest honeymoon because the army was already on the move – Harry quipping that, like Wellington, he never took leave. Juana, a sheltered child reared in upper-class luxury, and educated in a convent, was instantly bundled into the life of an army wife during a long and arduous campaign. Even allowing for the hyperbole of two old friends, Harry and

Johnny Kincaid, later looking back and describing their dramatic day in Badajoz, there is no doubt that Juana was the most captivating young woman. Her later portraits do not suggest outstanding beauty, yet evidence abounds of her physical attractiveness, and her positive and joyful personality. She came from a large family but, sadly, we know virtually nothing about them. This was not helped by the fact that most Spaniards considered Harry and most of Wellington's forces as heretics. She was a descendant of the Ponce de Leon, the Knight of Romance, a Spanish adventurer and explorer. Her full name, Juana Maria de Los Dolores de Leon, illustrates her Hidalgo bloodline, belonging to one of the oldest Spanish, rather than Moorish, families. The family's considerable affluence derived from their olive groves, but this severely reduced as the French cut down the trees.

The background to Harry's fateful meeting with Juana in Badajoz lay in Wellington's campaign. Since the start of what we now call the Napoleonic Wars in 1793, Napoleon had conquered most of Europe, but in Spain, where his forces – divided between his brother, whom he had appointed king, and several bickering marshals – had been undermined by effective Spanish guerrilla activity. This had prompted the British to send an expedition to Lisbon. From here, Wellington was able to drive north-east, from his base behind the Torres Vedras lines, a series of natural and man-made barriers which stretched across the Lisbon peninsula between the Tagus and the Atlantic. Badajoz and further north, Ciudad Rodrigo, had been fought over by Wellington and the French Marshals Marmont, Junot and Soult during the previous two years. The two towns, which lay in the passes in mountainous and forested country, and which were crucial to Wellington's lines of communication, posed grave problems for large-scale troop movements, and were vital to the security of the whole area. In 1811, after fierce fighting, a British attack on Badajoz had been bloodily repulsed, leaving the town in the hands of the jubilant French defenders.

During the following year the Allies gained the advantage when French forces in Spain were weakened by the demands of Napoleon's invasion of Russia. Many seasoned troops were withdrawn to the eastern front and replaced by inexperienced conscripts, and increasingly powerful Spanish guerrilla attacks tied down French forces which should have been available to face Wellington. When several thousand French troops from the Ciudad Rodrigo area withdrew, he seized the initiative and, despite appalling weather conditions, moved against both Ciudad Rodrigo and Badajoz. In January 1812, Wellington took Ciudad Rodrigo after a brief siege, but with severe losses, including one of his best commanders, General 'Black Bob' Craufurd, with whom Harry Smith had been briefly imprisoned after the Buenos Aires debacle in 1807 (as will be described in the next chapter). Wellington was then able to turn his attention to Badajoz.

To put an operation of this nature into context, the Army had not taken part in sieges of this magnitude for many years. Siege work was dangerous and despised by infantrymen who had to do much of the hard navvying work due to a lack of Royal Engineers, and Sappers and Miners. Indeed, William Napier in his *History of the War in the Peninsula* wrote:

> The sieges carried on by the British in Spain were a series of butcheries, because the commonest materials and means necessary for their art were denied to the engineers ... It was strange and culpable that the British Government should send an engineer corps into the field so ill-organised and equipped that all the officers' bravery and zeal would not render it efficient.

Tools were in short supply as were the essential 24–pounder guns, so vital to battering breaches in the substantial defences. Troops were exposed to the cold and freezing rain, together with accurate enemy fire and the occasional swift sally from the fort. Kincaid described siege warfare as 'the double calling of grave-digger and game-keeper [with] ample employment for both the spade and the rifle.' Command and control was difficult because as many men as possible had to be thrown into the breaches, creating muddled communication, only solved by officers leading from the front with the inevitable casualties. The inhabitants of Badajoz had the unfortunate reputation of being pro-French due to the suspicion that they had helped the defence on the two previous abortive attacks by the British in 1811, and had not treated British wounded well after the nearby Battle of Talavera in 1809. Orders for what should happen after the town was captured were sketchy, as officers simply had not faced this situation before.

General Amand Phillippon, a very brave and resourceful soldier who had risen through the ranks, with substantial campaign experience at Austerlitz, Talavera and Cadiz, commanded the French garrison of Badajoz. He was, however, a realist and knew that he could not hold out indefinitely, but he hoped Marshal Marmont, concentrating at Salamanca, or Soult in the south, would relieve him within three or four weeks. He and his chief engineer, Colonel Lamare, set out to make Badajoz, with its natural defensive position and man-made obstacles, a very much tougher nut to crack than Ciudad Rodrigo.

The fortification of Badajoz was typical of the style of the brilliant military architect, Vauban, with its nine bastions, mutually supporting, and connected by huge walls. The river Guadiana to the north, and the smaller river Rivellas to the east, gave added protection and created problems for the attackers. Man-made defences of ditches and palisades, with mines and accurately sited angles of fire support, would seriously worry a soldier of today, let alone Wellington's troops, unassisted by twenty-first-century technology. The chevaux-de-frise, large pieces of wood embedded with spikes, sword blades, bayonets and long nails, which could be bolted into position or pulled across a gap at the last moment, make today's barbed-wire entanglements look comparatively tame. Wellington's men knew it but, being well aware of the time-frame and a desire to finish a thoroughly unpleasant job, coupled with a grudge against the inhabitants and thoughts of plunder, were keen to press on.

In simple terms, siege operations amounted to trenches or parallels being dug, along which guns could be brought up to battery positions from where they could engage the enemy and pound the defences. This would, hopefully, produce a breach through which the infantry could assault. An alternative, more medieval way was to climb the walls by ladder, or 'escalade'. This was easier said than done against strong outposts. Well-led cavalry sallies from the garrison against those digging the trenches and battery positions, and accurate defensive fire, caused delay and heavy casualties.

Wellington had available the 3rd, 4th and 5th Divisions, each of two brigades, a brigade consisting of three or four infantry battalions. He also had the famed Light Division which included two battalions of Harry Smith's 95th Rifles (later to become the Rifle Brigade). Thus,

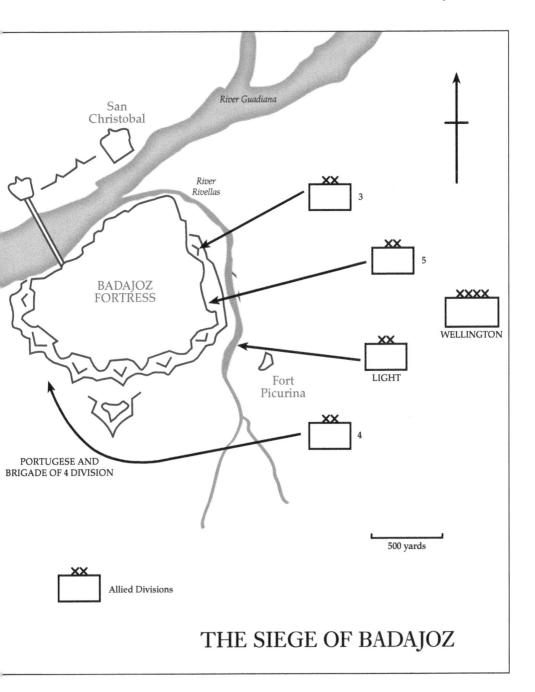

San
Christobal

*River Guadiana*

*River
Rivellas*

3

5

xxxx

WELLINGTON

BADAJOZ
FORTRESS

LIGHT

Fort
Picurina

4

PORTUGESE AND
BRIGADE OF 4 DIVISION

500 yards

Allied Divisions

# THE SIEGE OF BADAJOZ

twenty-three British infantry battalions and nine Portuguese faced Phillippon's 5,000 Frenchmen. However, the significance of the old military maxim that the defender has a three-to-one advantage over the attacker would not have been lost on either side.

Wellington decided to make his main assault on the south-east side of the town, first taking out Fort Picurina which lay on the eastern bank of the River Rivellas covering this approach. Twelve gun battery positions gave fire support to pound the defensive works and to provide covering fire for the assaulting troops. The Allies invested Badajoz on 16 March and launched their attack on Fort Picurina on 25 March; 500 men of the 3rd and Light Divisions led the assault. The bombardment had made a small breach in the defences, but the ladders were too short to reach the top of the walls. This and the withering French defensive fire caused heavy casualties – 300 killed or wounded.

Eleven days of bombardment and the frantic and dangerous digging of trenches continued until the main attack on the east side of the city on 6 April. The 4th and Light Divisions formed the left flank of the attack, with the 5th Division in the centre, and Picton's 3rd Division on the right flank. At the same time, two brigades from the 5th Division and the Portuguese made a diversionary attack on the north-west sector of the city. But, as seasoned soldiers know, no plan survives contact. The attacks, led by the aptly named Forlorn Hope – the assault party always oversubscribed by eager volunteers – were thrown back time and time again. Again the ladders were too short. Again the ditches filled up with the dead and dying. In the melee, command and control became impossible. Harry Smith, in the forefront of the Light Division attack, described the chaotic and lurid scenes as they tried to climb the escalades:

> When the head of the Light Division arrived at the ditch of the place it was a beautiful moonlight night. Old Alister Cameron was in command of four Companies of the 95th Regiment, extended along the counterscape to attract the enemy's fire, while the column planted their ladders. He came up to Barnard and said, 'Now my men are ready; shall I begin?' 'No, certainly not,' says Barnard. The breach and the works were full of the enemy, looking quietly at us, but not fifty yards off and most prepared,

although not firing a shot. So soon as our ladders were all ready posted, and the column in the very act to move and rush down the ladders, Barnard called out, 'Now, Cameron!' and the first shot from us brought down such a hail of fire as I shall never forget, nor ever saw before or since. It was most murderous. We flew down the ladders and rushed at the breach, but we were broken, and carried no weight with us, although every soldier was a hero. The breach was covered by a breastwork from behind, and ably defended on the top by chevaux-de-frises of sword-blades, sharp as razors, chained to the ground; while the ascent to the top of the breach was covered with planks with sharp nails in them. However, devil a one did I feel at this moment. One of the officers of the forlorn hope, Lieut. Taggart of the 43rd, was hanging on my arm – a mode we adopted to help each other up, for the ascent was most difficult and steep. A Rifleman stood among the sword-blades on the top of one of the chevaux-de-frises. We made a glorious rush to follow, but, alas! in vain. He was knocked over. My old captain, O'Hare, who commanded the storming party, was killed. All were awfully wounded except, I do believe, myself and little Freer of the 43rd. I had been some seconds at the revêtement of the bastion near the breach, and my red-coat pockets were literally filled with chips of stones splintered by musket-balls. Those not knocked down were driven back by this hail of mortality to the ladders. At the foot of them I saw poor Colonel Macleod with his hands on his breast – the man who lent me his horse when wounded at the bridge on the Coa. He said, 'Oh, Smith, I am mortally wounded. Help me up the ladder.' I said, 'Oh no, dear fellow!' 'I am,' he said; 'be quick!' I did so, and came back again. Little Freer and I said, 'Let us throw down the ladders; the fellows shan't go out.' Some soldiers behind said, 'D— your eyes, if you do we will bayonet you!' and we were literally forced up with the crowd ... So soon as we got on the glacis [the brickwork sloping defensive plate], up came a fresh Brigade of the Portuguese of the 4th Division. I never saw any soldiers behave with more pluck. Down into the ditch we all went again, but the more we tried to get up, the more we were destroyed. The 4th Division followed us in marching up to the breach, and they made a most uncommon noise. Both Divisions were fairly beaten back; we never carried either breach.

By midnight not a single British or Portuguese soldier had penetrated the defences, and the ditches overflowed with the dead and dying. Even the ebullient Smith was close to despair. Then to their amazement, they heard Allied bugle calls from within the city. Ironically, having spent weeks on creating breaches in the town walls, the successful assaults were actually made by escalade. Picton's 3rd Division in the north-east had crossed the River Rivellas and, despite fierce French opposition, managed to scale the walls, but not to gain an entrance. The ladders were too short in many cases and men had to stand on each other's shoulders to reach the top of the walls. Colonel Ridge of the 5th Foot (later the Northumberland Fusiliers) led the charge which broke the enemy's resolve but cost him his life. (He was reputed to be the first of Wellington's men into Badajoz.) In contrast to the repulse of the earlier attacks, the diversionary attack on the north-west sector by the brigades from the 5th and Portuguese Divisions, in spite of initially losing their way,broke in and effectively turned the French defences. Their success galvanized the other attackers to a final desperate and ultimately successful effort, but such was the strength of the defences that the 4th and Light Divisions were still unable to penetrate the walls until first light. Then the breaches were carried and there followed several hours of murderous hand-to-hand fighting. As the Allies broke in, General Phillippon rapidly withdrew his troops to the San Christobal fortress on the north bank of the River Guadiana, and at 7.00am on 7 April 1812 surrendered the city. Then the mayhem began.

# Chapter 2

# Early Life
# June 1787 to February 1812

'I will make you a Rifleman, a Green Jacket,' said General William
Stewart to the seventeen-year-old Harry Smith who was on duty at
a review held by the General in the spring of 1805. Thus Harry
started his military career: no physical or academic tests, no interview
and, importantly, no expensive purchase. Under the stresses of the
Napoleonic Wars almost any young man who wished to serve and could
read and write properly would have had little difficulty in obtaining a
Commission. Not wealth nor land but literacy was the key, before
education had extended to the whole population. This was the great
social divide. However, to obtain a Commission in a particular regiment,
purchase might well have been necessary. The General, to whom Harry,
then in the local Whittlesey Yeomanry as his temporary orderly, clearly
identified his potential.

Small in stature but an excellent horseman, Harry had been educated
as well as his father, the local surgeon, could afford, together with his ten
brothers and sisters. Harry's birthplace in St Mary's Street, Whittlesey,
is now called Aliwal House (photo 2). Although pretty unprepossessing,
it does have a plaque on the wall with the incorrect year of his birth,
1788 (photo 3). It is said that he was uncertain of this, but it is quite clear
from a copy of the parish register in the Whittlesey Museum, Harry was
born in 1787 (photo 1). In Harry's time, the east end of the south aisle
of St Mary's Church was partitioned off and used as a schoolroom. It
was here that he was educated by the Reverend George Burgess, then

curate, who survived to welcome him back to Whittlesey in 1847 on his triumphant return after the Battle of Aliwal. This part of the church, having been restored in 1862 as a memorial to him, is known even today as 'Sir Harry's Chapel'. It is now in a fairly neglected state and used mainly, it would seem, for storage. However, there is a significant memorial to Harry there, including a sword hanging underneath, which would seem anything but decorative. Also in the church are memorials to his parents, a nephew and the family vault. Harry's education and his standing as a gentleman were enough for the 95th Rifles and he joined the Regiment at Brabourne Lees on 18 August 1805. It has been said that Harry had difficulties in the Regiment as his brother officers were more aristocratic and had more money than he did, although there is no evidence of this. In fact, when Harry joined there were fifty-three fellow subaltern officers in the Regiment, none of whom had a title. In 1809 there were 140 peers or sons of peers among 10,000 officers on full pay, excluding the foreign regiments and veteran battalions. The fact that Eton, Harrow, Westminster, Rugby and Winchester provided only 283 officers between them suggests it was not the rich and privileged who dominated the officer corps. One officer in twenty was commissioned through the ranks. Harry – ever a spendthrift – did have financial problems for the rest of his life but, given the thoroughly inadequate rates of pay and haphazard administration of the Army, so did many of his friends.

Promotion, in those days, was often by purchase into vacancies or through exemplary behaviour in battle. Patronage also existed but was gradually going out of favour. There were no awards for gallantry but combat was eagerly sought for professional advancement into the gaps caused by casualties or the chance of promotion through distinguishing oneself. For these reasons, there was never a shortage of volunteers for the Forlorn Hope (the leading assault troops through any breach in enemy defences, or those out in front of a defensive line to take the first impact of the attack and identify the main enemy thrust). If you survived that, and few did, promotion was a certainty. However, luck was on Harry's side as a vacancy occurred in the next rank up when the Regiment formed a 2nd Battalion in the summer of 1805. The 95th was very popular and recruited easily from the Militia. The Ballot Act of

1802 stipulated that all men between the ages of eighteen and forty were liable to be drafted into the Militia, and some felt that rather than remain endlessly training in England to repel an invasion which, after Trafalgar, was unlikely to happen, they might as well join the Regular Army. In 1805, when the Regiment required fresh recruits after the Corunna campaign, 1,282 from the Militia volunteered. With a loan from his father, Harry was gazetted Lieutenant on 15 September 1805. As Harry put it in his autobiography: 'twenty-seven steps were obtained by £100,' i.e. by purchase, he had jumped his fellow second lieutenants. He was even more pleased when he was quickly appointed Adjutant of a detachment of three companies of the 2nd Battalion which, in the summer of 1806, was ordered to depart for South America.

The South American operation was a hare-brained, ill-thought-out scheme instigated by the early success of the maverick Admiral Home Popham who, in early 1806, had taken it upon himself to seize Buenos Aires from the Spaniards. This incident really smacked of little more than a privateering affair to wrest gold, territory and influence from the Spanish. It was ill-coordinated and no attention had been paid to its follow-up or long-term aims. However, a small British army of occupation was subsequently imposed on Buenos Aires under Colonel Beresford.

To compound this military frolic, in October 1806, Brigadier General 'Black Bob' Craufurd of the 95th was given orders from 10 Downing Street to take four battalions of Infantry of the Line and five companies of the 95th to gain a footing on the west coast of South America, with a view to opening commercial opportunities with the interior. The aim of the expedition was to capture the seaports and fortresses, and to reduce the Province of Chile. The orders inferred that, from the success at Buenos Aires, his force was 'probably adequate' for the job. He was warned, however, not to go beyond Chile or to attack Peru and Lima. It was suggested that having sailed with Admiral Murray's fleet either eastwards via New South Wales or westwards via Cape Horn, he should attack Valparaiso, a key town in Chile. The orders continued: 'On your arrival at the West Coast of South America, much must be left to your joint discretion in respect to the precise plan of operations which you are to pursue.' Having subdued Chile, he was instructed to treat the inhabitants rather better than their previous Spanish overlords did and establish communications 900 miles across the Andes Mountains with Beresford in Buenos Aires.

In the meantime, the Spaniards had easily retaken Buenos Aires and sent Beresford on his way, which meant that Craufurd's orders, luckily for all, were rescinded. He was instructed instead to join Sir Samuel Auchmuty off the east coast of South America and come under command of the inept General Whitelocke, who was later to be court-martialled, and his second-in-command, Lieutenant General Leveson-Gower, who certainly should have been. Sensibly, Auchmuty decided to establish a bridgehead in Monte Video before moving south into Buenos Aires. The assault on the well-defended Monte Video was Harry's first experience of battle. He wrote:

Upon the 20th [January 1807] the Spanish garrison made a most vigorous sortie in three columns, and drove in our outposts, a heavy and general attack lasted for near two hours, when the enemy were driven to the very walls of the place. The Riflemen were particularly distinguished on this occasion. The siege of Monte Video was immediately commenced and upon the morning of the 3rd of February, the breach being considered practicable, a general assault was ordered in two columns, the one upon the breach, the other an escalade. Both ultimately succeeded ... The breach was only wide enough for three men to enter abreast, and when upon the top of the breach there was a descent into the city of twelve feet. Most of the men fell, and many were wounded by each other's bayonets. When the head of the column entered the breach, the main body lost its communications or was checked by the tremendous fire. Perceiving the delay, I went back and conducted the column to the breach, when the place was immediately taken. The slaughter in the breach was enormous owing to the defence being perfect, and its not being really practicable. The surrender of this fortress put the English in the possession of this part of the country.

Harry was not to enjoy the euphoria of surviving his first exposure to hostile fire for long, as he was immediately struck low by fever and dysentery. He was cared for, curiously, by a Spanish family from whom he learned his rudimentary Spanish, which was later to stand him in such good stead. He clearly loved the family and they him, urging him to marry one of their daughters, with a substantial dowry of as many oxen as he wished and a house in the country. He politely declined and rejoined, still as Adjutant, Craufurd's force of the five rifle companies of the 1st Battalion of the 95th and the original three companies of the 2nd Battalion with whom he had embarked.

Initially the attack on Buenos Aires, led by Craufurd's light troops, began well and the Spaniards were driven into the centre of the city. Then, instead of being allowed to press home his advantage, Craufurd was inexplicably halted by General Leveson-Gower and his force weakly withdrawn, while General Whitelocke could not be found. Encouraged by this, the citizens of Buenos Aires took to their flat rooftops to fire down on the subsequent attacking waves and enfiladed the British from well-sited fire positions along the streets, which were built on a right-angled grid pattern. Unaccountably, General Whitelocke forbade his soldiers to load their weapons for the assault – one of the charges at his subsequent court-martial. The attack began to crumble and Craufurd's men, including Harry, were outnumbered and surrounded at the San Domingo Convent (photo 23). Craufurd had no option but to surrender. It was said that, while no blame attached to him for this debacle, he never forgave himself, let alone Whitelocke, at whose court-martial he was a witness. Crauford was evermore a 'driven' man, dying heroically leading his men at Ciudad Rodrigo in 1812. Harry's views were understandable:

> Thus terminated one of the most sanguinary conflicts Britons were ever engaged in, and all owing to the stupidity of the General-in-Chief and General Leveson-Gower. Liniers, a Frenchman by birth, who commanded the defence, treated us prisoners tolerably well, but he had little to give us to eat, his citadel not being provisioned for a siege. We were three or four days in his hands, when, in consequence of the disgraceful convention entered into by General Whitelocke, who agreed to evacuate the territory altogether and to give up the fortress of Monte Video, we were released. The army re-embarked with all

dispatch and sailed to Monte Video. Our wounded suffered dreadfully, many dying from slight wounds in the extremity of lockjaw.

Whitelocke was subsequently cashiered in March 1808 having been found guilty of six of the seven charges against him.

On 12 July 1807, Harry sailed for England and, enduring the dangers and difficulties of sailing in those days, returned, aged still only nineteen, to his beloved family in Whittlesey.

Harry had two months' leave before rejoining the Regiment at Colchester where, to his delight, in the light of his combat experience in South America, he was given command of a company. By all accounts, this company was pretty rough, although probably typical of the times. There is however a mystery – why should soldiers who were recruited from the dregs of society, were far from patriotic, and who were neglected and badly treated by their government and population, fight so well under incredibly harsh conditions? There was no doubt that the British soldier was well up to any of his opposite numbers on the Continent, and there is no evidence that it was the fear of the lash or gibbet that sent him again and again into a breach or line of enemy. It has been suggested that one reason was the confidence the soldiers felt in Wellington's personal leadership. While he strongly disapproved of senior officers exposing themselves to enemy fire by being too far forward, he obeyed no such stricture himself and, consequently, was relatively well known and recognized down to a very low level. Wellington himself said, 'When I come myself, the soldiers think that what they have to do is the most important, since I am there, and all will depend on their exertions.Of course, these are increased in proportion, and they will do for me what, perhaps, no one else can make them do.' However, for most, an additional important factor was the pride they felt in their regiment. In many ways, the Regiment represented all that they lacked as social outcasts: home, family and friends. It gave them the security and stability which was so lacking elsewhere in their lives. Additionally, the quality of the regiments depended on the relationship between the officers and their men. In Regulations for the Rifle Corps it was laid down that:

Every inferior, whether officer or soldier, shall receive the lawful commands of his senior with deference and respect, and shall execute them to the best of his power. Every superior in his turn, whether he be an officer or non-commissioned officer, shall give his orders in the language of moderation and of regard to the feelings of the individual under his command; abuse, bad language and blows being positively forbidden in the Regiment.

Most of the officers, in addition to courage, well understood the art of leadership.

Harry's generation had grown up knowing nothing but a state of war with France. Today our servicemen and women may be sent willy-nilly to the Balkans, Iraq or Afghanistan in support of supposed national or international policies; similarly, Harry found himself in a short space of time in Spain, in South America and in the Baltic. In 1807, just when he was returning from South America, Britain faced a very severe threat. Napoleon had defeated Russia and had dictated the Treaty of Tilsit, by which he intended to amalgamate the navies of Denmark, Sweden, Russia and France in a major challenge to Britain's naval supremacy and its crucial trade with the Baltic. During the summer of 1807, within weeks of the Tilsit Treaty, Britain sent a powerful force of battleships and frigates, and 25,000 troops, to attack Copenhagen.

Outrageously, the British demanded that the Danes hand over their fleet, a demand that was instantly rejected. Lord Cathcart, commanding the expedition, then landed the majority of the troops – many of them Germans from Hanover. While the warships faced Copenhagen from the sea, the army, with powerful reinforcements of artillery, surrounded the city from the land side. This totally illegal act against a neutral country caused serious concern to many of the commanders and officers involved. One naval captain deplored it as totally unjustifiable, while a doctor serving in a battleship said he felt for the disconsolate inhabitants while the army reduced the land around the city to a melancholy waste.

At the end of August 1807, Sir Arthur Wellesley, commanding a division surrounding Copenhagen, and already showing those skills which came to fruition in the Peninsula, decisively defeated the main Danish forces at Kiogo, just south of the city, and took 1,000 prisoners. In the aftermath of that victory Wellesley's troops desecrated the neatly kept cemeteries, and – with shades of Badajoz – grabbed jewels and tore earrings from the local women. Wellesley's victory prompted another demand for the Danes to surrender their fleet and when this was refused on 2 September, the British started a major bombardment of the city – one of the finest in northern Europe. The bombardment started with salvoes of shells and red-hot cannon balls from the battleships, as well as the new-fangled Congreve rockets, which continued for three days and nights. In the end the city was almost completely destroyed, including the cathedral, famous churches, the royal palace and all the major buildings in the capital. An observer wrote: 'We used to sit up at night watching shells and rockets flying through the air like so many blazing comets.' On 7 September, the Danes gave in. The city had suffered about 2,000 casualties, mostly civilians including women and children. Many eyewitnesses among the British soldiers graphically described the appalling suffering of the people. The people of Copenhagen were dignified in defeat, but when the British seized over fifty ships and naval stores enough to fill ninety transports, they were absolutely outraged.

The attack on Copenhagen proved to be a valuable taste of war for the military and naval forces which took part, including the 28th and 75th of Foot (later the Gloucester Regiment and Gordon Highlanders respectively) and many artillery units, but for Denmark it was an undeserved and total disaster, with the destruction of their thriving overseas trade and the loss of Norway, over which they held sway, to Sweden in war reparation. In England the Government came under strong criticism from both Houses of Parliament. Wilberforce, at the height of his power from the anti-slavery issue at this time, claimed that our national reputation was besmirched, while many of the commanders who took part deplored what they had been forced to do. One stated, 'There is no shame left.' Harry's unit only took part in what was an ineffective follow-up to the main action and was positioned further north along the Swedish coast near Gothenburg. Active as ever, when his troops were briefly landed, he organized an athletics contest and managed to win the long jump with a leap of 19 feet. The whole of the Copenhagen expedition remains a good early example of the forces' reaction to an unjust war. For many commanders and troops alike, though, this operation provided a dress rehearsal for what was to come in Spain.

By 1808, Spanish guerrillas – in contrast to the regular Spanish forces – operating across the whole of the Peninsula from Aragon to Portugal, had inflicted serious damage on the French armies. This was a major factor in the British decision to mount an expedition to Portugal. Thus Harry arrived there in August 1808, just as Sir Arthur Wellesley – before he became the Duke of Wellington – won the Battle of Vimiero. Despite this British victory, the French were given an absurdly generous settlement under the Convention of Cintra, including the repatriation of 20,000 French troops in British ships. This caused an outcry at home, but fortunately it was arranged by the second-rate General Dalrymple and did not harm the career of Wellesley.

After this debacle, Harry was attached to the forces of Sir John Moore as they advanced northwards. Because of his good knowledge of Spanish, Harry was much in demand, obtaining local rations and acquiring billets, in addition to reconnoitring river crossings and possible objectives. However, during November, the Spanish resistance to the French collapsed and Moore was driven from Spain in December 1808. Though he heroically evacuated all but a few thousand stragglers from his army, and saved both Cadiz and Lisbon, he was killed at Corunna on 16 January 1809. Harry was heavily involved in rearguard actions covering the retreat of demoralized and disorganized soldiers. He was appalled by the behaviour of many of them, despite the fact that they had only just thrashed the French at Corunna. Harry wrote: 'The army embarked the following day ... oh the filthy state we were all in; we lost our baggage at Calcavellos; for three weeks we had no clothes but those on our backs; we were literally covered and almost eaten up with vermin, most of us suffering from ague and dysentery, every man a living still active skeleton.' He himself was no exception and when his Commanding Officer, Colonel Beckwith, saw him disembarking at Portsmouth, he ordered him 'with a warmth of heat equalling the thunder of his voice' to return home and take leave of absence. Thus, once again, Harry was nurtured and rejuvenated in the loving care of his family.

Two months later, he rejoined the 95th and embarked for Portugal on 25 May. By now, Wellesley had landed again at Lisbon, which had never

Toulouse

Corunna

Bayonne
Nivelle

FRANCE

Santander

Tarbes

San Sebastian

Vitoria

Vigo

Calcavellos

Pamplona

Oporto

PORTUGAL

Burgos

Palencia

Valladolid

Barcelona

Salamanca

SPAIN

Ciudad Rodrigo

Sabugal

Fuentes de Onoro

Busaco

MADRID

Talavera

Toledo

Valenica

LISBON
Torres Vedras

Badajoz

Albuera

Seville

THE
PENINSULA
CAMPAIGN

Cadiz

Gibraltar

been abandoned by its British defence force. Together with Portuguese and Spanish allies, and, hopefully, favourable conditions, he planned to go on the offensive and clear the Peninsula of the French. General Craufurd was now commanding the Light Division with vigour and strong discipline. Long marches ensued – for instance, Harry quotes one of 56 miles achieved in twenty-eight hours. Modern soldiers are, rightly, proud of the weights they carry over long distances, but the Peninsula men also carried 70 to 80 lb. A knapsack might contain two shirts, two pairs of stockings, one pair of shoes, three brushes, box of blacking, razor, soap box and strap, an extra pair of trousers, a mess tin, centre tin and lid, haversack and canteen, greatcoat and blanket, a filled powder flask, a ball bag containing thirty loose balls, a small wooden mallet used to hammer the ball into the rifle muzzle; in addition, they wore a belt and pouch, the latter containing fifty rounds of ammunition and sword belt, and carried a rifle. There was also equipment to be divided up among the section of eight men, such as four billhooks weighing 6 lb each – thus every second day a man would have to carry one of these. All this was in poorly fitted packs, uncomfortable clothing not designed for the Spanish summer and boots which did not have a left and right and probably did not fit properly anyway. Tents were not issued until 1813.

While the Light Division made its forced marches, Wellesley's main force was advancing up the valley of the River Tagus and in July 1809 reached Talavera. Here, with a strong Spanish contingent, they faced an almost equal number of French, under King Joseph and Jourdan. The battle, from the 27th to the 29th, was one of the bloodiest of the Peninsula War, with both sides losing over 5,000 casualties, but was properly seen as a British and Spanish victory at home, where public relations were as important then as they are now. In recognition of his achievements, Wellesley was awarded a well-earned Viscountcy.

On the battlefield, bodies quickly putrefied in the heat and produced a gagging stench. An effort was made to collect the dead and burn them but this proved so unacceptable to those carrying out the task that mass graves were dug for both sides (these were unearthed in 1990 when a by-pass was built round the north of Talavera). The Light Division reached Talavera the day after the battle and was welcomed by the exhausted survivors. Relying on what they could scrounge from the countryside, Harry and his men did not live well but, again, thanks to his Spanish, he was able to barter and buy exorbitantly priced bread from the Spanish soldiers. Sickness, mainly dysentery, was rife but Harry managed, somehow, to obtain some hounds and went coursing, which added meat to the pot, but, even better, kept him fit and well through exercise and fresh air.

Once, when out of camp, Harry's group came across some local bandits who they initially scared off with a lot of noise, pretending to be part of a larger force, and, since they had no ball ammunition, by firing buttons pulled off their coats. The bandits, not fooled for very long, soon put Harry and the rest to flight. Characteristically, however, Harry was not going to put up with this, so he made some enquiries and, discovering that this was a band of about twenty, led by a notorious Catalan, decided to deal with them. He assembled a motley bunch of about ten soldiers and set out after the brigands. They found them in a stable attached to a small Roman Catholic chapel and, after a quick reconnaissance, Harry and his men carried out a silent attack. Catching the enemy by surprise, they captured all the bandits, including their captain, a number of horses and the leader's fine dagger, which Harry sent home to his father as a present. As the adrenaline wore off, Harry became nervous that his little private expedition – entirely on his own initiative – would incur the wrath of General 'Black Bob' Craufurd. However, all was well: some of the bandits, being well-known offenders were sentenced to life on the galleys, the sale of captured horses provided forty Spanish dollars for each of his men and Harry kept the leader's fine horse, as well as being given credit for ridding the countryside of these marauders.

Meanwhile Wellington, aware that the French were closing in, and totally disillusioned with Spanish promises of aid, fell back into Portugal and ordered the secret construction of the celebrated Lines of Torres Vedras. Harry was far from idle and, while continuing to go coursing, was put in charge of what we would now call a close reconnaissance team, by General Craufurd. This was just up his street. He was given a sergeant and twelve troopers of the 1st German Hussars to penetrate the French defences and gather information. Never two nights in the same place, Harry's small team had many skirmishes. One night, when observing a ford over the River Agueda, two of his Polish sentries deserted to the French. Fearing that their position was now compromised and that they were therefore very vulnerable, Harry's sergeant roused him from his half-sleep. They immediately pulled back to the rear of a small village, remaining in the saddle for the rest of the night. When, at dawn, they saw about fifty French dragoons wending their way down to the ford on the other side of the river, Harry ordered the village headman, the alcalde, to assemble about a hundred of his villagers, armed with their bullock-driving whips and long sticks. Splitting them into two groups in the lee of the hills, with only the tops of their sticks showing so that they looked as though they were bayonets, Harry and his men rode up and down furiously, creating dust and noise to create the impression of a large force. Having tentatively sent half their men over the ford, the French then thought the better of it and rapidly withdrew. Harry instantly became the hero of the village, which he had saved from a ransacking.

A small incident then took place that very much endeared his German Hussars to Harry. He was manning one of the vedettes, or forward observation posts, well out in front of the Division. He had been there all day without any sustenance, only being allowed to take his horse and telescope with him and, by evening, was vainly looking for the arrival of his orderly bringing him something to eat and drink. One of the Hussars noticed his anxiety and asked him what was wrong. Harry explained that it was all right for the troopers who were relieved every two hours, but he had been there since daybreak with nothing to eat or drink all day. With that the trooper dismounted and told Harry to get on his horse and keep watch, while he undid the valise behind the saddle, and took out some bacon, coffee and sugar which he promptly brewed up. He then laid out a tin cup, knife and fork on a clean towel and invited Harry to eat. Harry fell to with relish while the Hussar, having remounted, watched him with a smile. When Harry's soldier servant, who had got lost, eventually arrived with the food and half a bottle of wine, this was immediately handed over to Harry's benefactor whose conduct he never forgot.

However, what was to come was very different from these minor skirmishes. In the spring of 1810, Wellington faced the very real possibility of losing Portugal to Marshal Massena, one of Napoleon's best generals. The elite troops of Craufurd's Light Division were heavily involved in actions which, although relatively minor, nevertheless were vital to the protection of the main Army. This was no more so than during the month's skirmishing on the line of the River Coa. While Wellington depended on the competence of his generals, Craufurd's impetuosity must have tried him. Having been ordered to remain as long as possible on the enemy side of a bridge over the Coa, to impose delay and then withdraw when the enemy arrived in force, Craufurd rashly positioned his men further out where they fell prey to a heavy French force. But for the distinguished leadership of Colonel Beckwith of the 95th, this could have turned into a real disaster.

During this incident Harry was in the rearguard, protecting the bridge crossing, and in constant contact with the enemy. Luckily the bridge was stoutly held by the 95th, but Harry and his brother, Tom, were severely wounded. With a ball in his ankle joint, severing his Achilles tendon, for Harry the war was over, temporarily at least. He managed to hitch a relatively comfortable lift to the rear in a sedan chair. Nonetheless, although clearly in much pain, he had no intention of remaining 'walking wounded' for long and, when he heard of the withdrawal of his Regiment to the Lines of Torres Vedras, he determined to rejoin them as soon as possible. This was not as easy as he thought and while he was allowed to leave, he was put in command of some 600 'sick, lame and lazy' who were being sent up to the front as reinforcements. As soon as he could, he palmed them off onto other officers and rejoined his Colonel, Sidney Beckwith. The latter, seeing Harry was in no real state to fight, made him his ADC, which did not, however, prevent General Craufurd from detailing him, as he knew the roads so well, to take a dispatch to the Duke. However, the documents took so long to draft that the General told him not to hang around waiting for them any longer and he would send a Dragoon orderly in due course. It was just as well, as Harry heard later that the poor fellow was subsequently ambushed by the enemy.

No warfare is entirely without humour and the Peninsula was no exception. Harry and his Colonel were standing, talking, in their camp when it began to rain heavily. As they watched, a rifleman knocked out the end of a large wine barrel and crept inside to shelter. But he had not secured it properly and it took off, rolling down the hill with the man inside. The soldier was unhurt but Beckwith and Harry could hardly control their mirth as the shaken individual emerged.

As Colonel Beckwith was required in Lisbon, it seemed a good opportunity for Harry to go with him and have his wound treated. The ball was still in his ankle and had 'sloughed' – or in other words, unsurprisingly, it had started to go septic. There was then a certain amount of indecision amongst the surgeons as to whether they should take the ball out or cut his leg off. One of them, Brownrigg, said, 'If it were my leg, out should come the ball.' Harry enthusiastically agreed, lifted his leg up and said, 'There it is; slash away.' One can imagine the pain with no anaesthetic, of course. The ball was jagged and heavily embedded in the leg, to such an extent the forceps the doctors were using broke. Harry's great friend, George Simmons, who was also wounded, was watching. When the surgeons needed some swabs and bandages, Harry invited George to tear up one of his shirts. George took one look at it and refused as it was 'a pity; it is a good shirt'. Harry was not pleased as his leg was aching and 'smoking' from a wound four or five inches long. Nevertheless, he appears to have recovered rapidly and, before the wound was even healed, had rejoined his Colonel on 6 March 1811.

On arrival, Harry found one of the company commanders had fallen sick and so he implored the Colonel to be allowed to command the company. Although lame and in considerable pain Harry was given command, despite having to remain, uncomfortably, in the saddle for some considerable time. There was much fighting and considerable losses were sustained: Jack Stewart, a friend of Harry's, was shot through the lungs; another was shot off his horse and a lieutenant was killed when actually talking to Harry. Later, to his astonishment, Harry was appointed Brigade Major of the 2nd Light Brigade, effectively the executive officer of a brigade of three or more battalions. The Brigade was commanded by a lazy old Guardsman, Drummond, who clearly had his priorities right – when Harry asked for orders he said, 'It is your duty to post the picquets, and mine to have a damned good dinner for you every day.'

The British gradually pushed the French over the border into Spain and eventually into the well-fortified town of Ciudad Rodrigo. Sadly, Wellington's generals were not all of the stamp of Moore, Craufurd and Tom Picton. There were those such as Brent Spencer who were, at best, indecisive, who allowed the French to escape from Almeida after Wellington's success at Fuentes de Onoro; and others, like Erskine, who eventually committed suicide in Lisbon, who were merely drunk and incompetent.

In the winter of 1811, Harry and the rest of the army found themselves on the frontier, keeping Ciudad Rodrigo under observation. One evening Harry was chatting to General Craufurd and another of his friends, Tom Bell, when a Dragoon rode up with a request from General Lowry Cole for an officer who knew the roads to guide his Division to their next position at dusk. Harry, with his intimate knowledge of the area, was detailed to go. On arrival at Cole's headquarters, the General asked him if he knew the way. Harry sarcastically retorted, 'I suppose I should not have been sent if I had not.' He was actually not that confident in the dark, with masses of soldiers milling about, and it did not help having the anxious Cole continually enquiring whether they were on the right track. Harry said, 'General Cole, if you will let me alone, I will conduct your Division; if you thus attract my attention, I cannot.' It was a nasty moment, particularly as Harry had to gallop ahead to verify he did actually have the right road. To his relief, he found it and as the head of the column reached it, he did not hang about. With a 'Good night, General' he galloped off into the night with Cole's shouts to come back sounding in his ears. (It did, however, have a happy ending: Harry became the General's AQMG – chief divisional administrative officer – after Waterloo, then, much later served under him in the Cape when Cole was Governor.)

On 8 January 1812, a fresh chapter was opened in the Peninsula War with the start of the siege of Ciudad Rodrigo. The four Divisions (1st, 3rd, 4th and Light) took it in turns to be on duty besieging the town. It was cold, unpleasant and hazardous work involving, every fourth day, a 9-mile march in to the objective, crossing the River Agueda, and a return march out the following day. The vital hill overlooking the town initially fell to the Allies and on 16 January the lesser intervening high ground was taken. With guns blasting two main breaches on the 19th, the citadel was taken that night with fierce fighting. By so doing, Wellington secured his northern route and essential lines of communication into Spain, and could turn his attention to Badajoz.

Harry, as Senior Subaltern of the 95th, volunteered himself as commander of the Forlorn Hope. He was swiftly rebuffed by Craufurd who told him in no uncertain terms that he was a Brigade Major – and by implication he should get on with his proper job – and leave that sort of thing to younger officers. To Harry's disgust another subaltern, Lieutenant Gurwood, was given the job. Gurwood was knocked unconscious in the assault and, coming to later, managed to find the French Governor of the town and relieve him of his sword. Harry was nevertheless in the thick of it and, hatless and with his clothes singed, was taken for a Frenchman by an enormous Grenadier of the 88th (later the Connaught Rangers). He was grabbed by the throat but just had enough breath to swear at him roundly in unmistakable English, thus saving his life.

Sadly, Harry's heroes, General Craufurd, Colonel Colborne and Colonel Mackinnon, were not so lucky. Craufurd was hit in the spine and died in great pain. After his burial in the breach where he fell, his soldiers marched back to camp straight through a large freezing pond in silent tribute to their beloved leader, who, as one of his 'severities' during training, would roar 'Sit down in it, Sir, sit down in it' if a soldier stepped over a puddle. Mackinnon, Commanding Officer of the 88th, who had led his men with the words 'Rangers of Connaught! It is not my intention to spend any powder this evening. We'll do this business with the cold iron', was blown up near Harry. (Dan Mackinnon was a very popular leader and well known throughout the Army as a practical joker. He once impersonated the Duke of York at a banquet and dived headlong into a bowl of punch. Another time, when Wellington was visiting a convent, he impersonated a nun.) Colborne was hit in the right shoulder and though he was operated on, the ball remained in his arm. Months later he complained of a pain four inches from where the ball had entered. The surgeons again opened up his arm and removed the ball, which had embedded itself in the bone. The operation was so painful that Colborne put his watch beside him on the operating table and only allowed the doctors to work for five minutes at a time. It was three or four days before they finally completed the operation. Nevertheless, in three weeks, Colborne was back commanding his Regiment in the Pyrenees, merely complaining that he only had use of his arm below the elbow.

For Harry, the gloomy aftermath of this sort of major battle was the execution of deserters. As Brigade Major, Harry had a supervisory role, but the detail was the Provost Marshal's, who had not organized the execution well and whose orders were unclear. Out of the eleven deserters kneeling by a mass grave, some were killed immediately but a few only wounded. Harry had to take charge, order the firing party to reload and dispatch the unfortunate individuals.

On 28 February 1812, Harry was promoted captain. Now Wellington could turn his attention to Badajoz where Harry and Juana would meet.

# Chapter 3

# Peninsula
## April 1812 to April 1814

We now return to the smoking devastation of Badajoz, the fall of which had such a dramatic effect on both commanders.

Wellington openly wept at the loss of the cream of his army – 5,000 casualties – and Napoleon, in a fury at the French defeat, turned his concentration almost exclusively to his campaign in Russia. During the siege, Wellington had realized that the French under Marmont were approaching, and as he moved north towards Ciudad Rodrigo and Salamanca, the rival armies moved in fairly close parallel, with just occasional skirmishes. As the armies approached Salamanca during June 1812, Wellington made several feints to lure the French into battle, but Marmont refused because reinforcements from their southern armies were on the way. Indeed, Wellington even considered abandoning Salamanca and retiring towards Portugal. At this time the two armies were evenly matched – 48,000 Allies to 50,000 French, and with a similar balance in heavy guns. On 22 July, Wellington, with most of his army lying in dead ground and unseen by the enemy, ordered two of his commanders, Pakenham and D'Urban, to move their units to his left flank. Marmont saw the dust clouds which this movement created and assumed that the Allies were retreating. He therefore wheeled his army round intending to attack the retreating enemy, unaware that in reality he was crossing in front of their main force. Wellington, realizing Marmont's mistake, immediately gave orders to attack, and in forty minutes the main French army was routed. Wellington's quip '40,000

French in forty minutes', did not tell the whole story and there were hard-fought battles during the rest of the day before the French were finally defeated. Wellington's quick decision when he was on the spot at a crucial moment in the battle secured the victory, as it had, and for the same reasons, as the timeless victory of Alexander the Great at Gaugamela.

Harry suffered severely from boils during this period and described the agony he went through when he was riding. When Salamanca fell, he had eleven excruciating boils and the army surgeon ordered him to stay in Salamanca for two weeks until they improved. Harry's brother Tom, who also served in the Headquarters, took over his duties, while Harry and Juana spent 'fourteen days of love and excitement' in Salamanca. The story of the boils is well known, but one wonders whether it was a kind gesture by the authorities to give the popular young couple a break from the rigours of campaigning. Almost immediately after their marriage, Juana had faced a serious problem. She had only ever ridden a donkey on a religious pilgrimage and now urgently needed to ride a horse. Harry, who always kept a number of horses and greyhounds, had a side-saddle made for his lovely new wife and allotted her a large but placid Portuguese horse. Juana, with her haughty Spanish attitude, and already prepared to clash with 'her Enrique', despised everything Portuguese and this horse in particular. During the march north towards Salamanca that August, she was crossing a river in a thunderstorm when the horse panicked, putting her in serious danger. She instantly refused to ride it again and demanded to ride a spirited Spanish thoroughbred called Tiny. To the delight of all the troops who watched admiringly, she quickly controlled Tiny and rode him thereafter. Harry wrote in his autobiography: 'It is difficult to say who was the proudest that morning ... horse, wife or Enrique (as I was always called), as she caracoled him about among the soldiers to their delight.' Her occasional flare-ups with Harry were always concluded with laughter and passionate embraces, and often they would lie in each other's arms under the stars.

Harry, as Brigade Major – a fairly senior staff officer – realized that he would have to leave Juana alone for long periods and entrusted her to the care of 'his trusty old groom West', who cared for her devotedly and slept nearby when Harry was away. She seems to have gained the affection and respect of both officers and men and there is no record of her being or feeling threatened. Harry wrote: 'The soldiers of the whole division loved her … and she would laugh and talk with all, which a soldier loves. Blackguards as many of the poor fellows were, there was not a man who would not have laid down his life to defend her.' Before a battle, West would take Juana to the rear – often against her strong protests. One night when he had cut green wheat to make her a mattress, and when she had to hold Tiny's rein all night, she found in the morning that the horse had eaten all her bed, 'to her juvenile amusement, for a creature so gay and vivacious, with all her sound sense, the earth never produced'.

It was a welcome rest but they were so short of money that they could not even afford to buy coffee. After fourteen days they had to ride 'some terrible distances for three or four days' and they caught up with the Division at the Guadarama Pass. This pass, the key to Madrid through centuries of war and civil war, was quickly overcome and the triumphal Allies marched unopposed into the city. Madrid, particularly, had resented Napoleon's arrogance in deposing their king, and the whole population turned out to give the British forces a joyful and ecstatic welcome. Soldiers and officers alike were showered with gifts, with flowers and with wine. Women in their eagerness to kiss the conquering heroes nearly pulled them off their horses, and even Spanish men grabbed the soldiers and kissed them – to the disgust of the British troops. What a contrast to their entry to Badajoz!

After the severe privations of the march, Harry and Juana were able to live well in luxurious accommodation near the city centre and even afford new clothes. In the evenings they enjoyed walking down the elegant Prado where Harry thought 'his Estramenha' outshone all the Spanish beauties. The celebrations continued for several weeks with the capital lit up every night, and Harry escorted his lovely young wife to dinners, dances and bullfights. With their fluent Spanish they were in great demand, both socially and professionally as interpreters.

After this all too brief interlude of joy and relaxation, the Light Division was left in Madrid, while Wellington, with three other divisions, marched north to attack Burgos. He laid siege to the town on 19

September 1812, but it was resolutely defended. He was short of siege artillery and once again heavy rain hampered operations. By the middle of October, French reinforcements were assembling to the north of the city and on 18 October 1812, Wellington decided to give up the siege and retreat to the west, claiming, correctly, that a good commander knew when to attack and when to retreat. Back in Madrid, rumours of retreat began to circulate. One night General Vandeleur, the Divisional Commander, despite Harry's fierce protestations, called out the whole Division, only to find that the majority of men were drunk. Morale fell, resentment increased, and men longed for the firm and confident hand of Wellington.

Wellington's previous experience of command in India proved to be a sound preparation for his task in the Peninsula. Although he was later renowned as a consummate politician and coalition leader, he honed those skills in the Peninsula with his prickly and demanding Portuguese allies, and the frequently uncooperative Spanish. After Salamanca and the occupation of Madrid, he was given command of the Spanish armies despite the antagonism of the *Cortes*, the Spanish Government.

In the face of a substantial French threat, all the Allied divisions joined up and began a long and wretched retreat back towards Ciudad Rodrigo, during which the Light Division fought a prolonged rearguard action. In Madrid, the Smiths had become friendly with a Spanish priest and when the retreat began, he begged for protection. Harry agreed, and soon his entourage included the usual horses and dogs as well as the padre – nicknamed Harry's Confessor. The padre proved useful and during the retreat, when the whole army suffered from cold, sickness and near starvation, he always seemed able to obtain little extras and luxuries. After the comfort of Madrid they soon had to put up with the severe privations of the march – one officer recording that he did not have his boots off for six days. Harry vividly described their sufferings and their desperate shortage of money. He had sold a horse for the substantial price of three Spanish doubloons – a small fortune – which Juana packed among his clothes in a portmanteau. But the doubloons were lost on the journey with the motion of the mule. Juana was distraught: 'Her horror, poor girl, is not to be described.' After the misery of several nights of wet clothes, 'out tumbled three doubloons ...

Oh, such joy and such laughing. We were so rich. We could buy bread and chocolate and sausages and eggs, and our little fortune carried us through to Ciudad Rodrigo, where money was paid to us.'

As the Allied divisions trudged doggedly on through the wet and the cold, Marshal Soult, an outstanding French commander, with nearly twice as many troops as Wellington, came close enough to threaten the retreat, and the Light Division had to fight some serious delaying actions. During one of these, at the crossing of a swollen river, Juana's spirited Spanish horse saved her by leaping up the bank. In contrast, the poor padre fell off his pony, which was drowned, but he was saved by the air trapped in his Spanish cloak. As he emerged, Harry joked that he might have been drawn for 'the Knight of the Woeful Countenance'. In this encounter Harry had sent Juana and the padre to the 52nd Regiment, who were not expected to be involved in the fighting. But with a sudden turn – typical of that sort of warfare – Juana found herself in the thick of a major action. This 'young and delicate creature' faced danger, cold, hunger and every privation, but she only once complained. This was when they were sleeping in the open, Harry fell asleep and cut her off from the warmth of the fire. He was well known for his entourage of horses, dogs and greyhounds – and the padre – but he also took on a few locals whom he could use as guides. One morning his friend, Charles Beckwith, came to borrow one, because the neighbouring 1st Division could not move off without a guide. It was this ability to cope with every situation which made Harry such a widely respected officer throughout the Peninsula forces. With the help of his guide, the Division quickly moved off and the French were unable to follow, so the Light Division had a long, unmolested march. Harry added, 'Yesterday the soldiers' life was one of misery, today all joy and elasticity.'

The soldiers always called Harry 'Mr Smith' and as the unit moved off after a skirmish, a wounded soldier called out, 'Mr Smith, do not leave me here.' The poor man had been wounded by a cannon shot and could not move. Harry knew him as a gallant soldier and immediately arranged for a tumbrel – a wagon for carrying a heavy gun – and the soldier was taken on. Sadly, he died shortly afterwards.

During the long and gruesome retreat from Madrid, the army lost several thousand to sickness and disease, but as they approached Ciudad Rodrigo their morale improved. They felt at home there and faced the agreeable prospect of living in proper winter quarters. The Smiths had a pleasant little house and Juana, 'full of animation and happiness', made it a warm and hospitable home, helped by the padre who proved to be an excellent cook. Harry went coursing, shooting or hunting nearly every afternoon, and usually returned with hares, duck or wild pig to augment the rations. Wellington himself, who ran a pack of foxhounds, often joined in the hunting and clearly enjoyed the company of his enthusiastic young officers.

Harry and Juana, able to converse easily with the local people, were drawn into many colourful social activities, including a local rustic wedding in which, traditionally, the guests gave valuable presents to the bride during a ritual dance. Juana learnt the dance and presented the bride with a doubloon, to the surprise and delight of the family. Harry spent many happy days hunting in the great cork, oak and chestnut forests. It is easy to forget how dependent officers were on their horses in those days because of course no other reasonable method of swift transport existed. Harry had started this particular part of the campaign with five 'capital horses', which one would have thought were enough, but only two of them turned out to be fit. Tiny, Juana's good little Arab horse, had received a serious injury from a collapsing bullock-manger (an immensely heavy timber construction), when the sharp-pointed end fell on his off fore-hoof. He became so lame he could hardly walk and was a significant loss to Juana. General Vandeleur now and then provided a horse for Harry, or he would have been in real trouble. Trying to help out, James Stewart, an old friend of Harry, lent him a very sound English hunter. However, he picked up a nail in his hind foot and was not fit to ride for months. Such problems with horses were quite common but Harry had to admit that, in winter quarters, his fit horses, because they were so few, had no real rest.

Once again, he and Juana enjoyed their contacts with the local people and often took part in rural village customs. They shared one traditional activity when the locals drove their pigs out into the forest and then flogged the trees to provide them with a special diet of nuts and acorns. When the pigs were killed, celebrations and feasts continued for days, during which the meat was cured, and enough sausages and black puddings were made to last for months. A particular local delicacy, usually eaten at breakfast, was pork boiled with salt, red peppers and garlic.

Caesar's *Gallic War* described hibernia when the legions went into winter quarters, and this tradition certainly continued into the Peninsula campaign. For officers, the winter meant a whirl of social activities and many days of hunting and coursing. Kincaid described how in winter quarters his unit took over a church for amateur theatricals, and he managed to make a comfortable bed from gorgeous clerical robes and trappings. Consequently, he was regularly cursed by the Bishop of Rodrigo. As usual the troops made the best of everything and kept up that well-known soldierly tradition that only a fool can be uncomfortable.

Harry's exuberant personality colours his writing and he often gives the impression that the divisions were one big happy family – but there is a darker side. *The Letters of Private Wheeler*, who served in the 51st (later the King's Own Yorkshire Light Infantry) in the campaign around Badajoz and Ciudad Rodrigo, paint a very different picture. Wheeler described the petty tyranny of autocratic and drunken colonels, who would set up drumhead courts martial for trivial offences and sentence men to 300 or even 500 lashes.

The army used the winter lull to overcome the ravages of the year's campaign. The rudimentary medical provision actively helped the many wounded and sick. During the long campaign of 1812 from Ciudad Rodrigo to Madrid and back, uniforms were reduced to tatters and boots were quickly worn out. Lacking later refinements, there were not left- or right-foot boots, but just boots which would fit either foot – useful when a man lost a leg. During the winter, reinforcements arrived to replace the many casualties, long-awaited uniforms appeared and back pay was made up. Among the reinforcements were some units of the Household Cavalry in splendid uniforms. The Light Bobs, as the Light Division were nicknamed, teased the newcomers, and proudly wore their ragged, worn-out kit – an attitude cheerfully echoed later in the 1940s Desert Campaign, when new arrivals were told to get their knees brown. Harry, always a spendthrift, received his back pay, but it barely covered his debts. His family was not wealthy, but occasionally his father, the surgeon from Whittlesey, would help him out.

In the spring of 1813, the armies waited expectantly for a new campaign to start, but presumably for security reasons little warning was ever given. On 21 May, the Light Division, after several months in winter quarters, received orders at midnight to leave at dawn the next day. The route to Palencia and thence to Vitoria, over 200 miles, took them over the same country they had trudged through in the grim retreat of the previous autumn, but the prospect of action created an atmosphere of joy and anticipation. Such was the pride and spirit in the Light Division that they were angry when another division was chosen to lead an assault, and units were overwhelmed with volunteers for the Forlorn Hope, many of whom expected to be killed, or in Kincaid's vivid phrase 'given a passport to eternity'.

The Division moved off in delightful weather and with plentiful supplies – 'the mainspring of happiness in a soldier's life' – and with the total confidence in Wellington's leadership. The French had destroyed a bridge over the Douro, a magnificent and fast-flowing river, but the veteran Light Division rapidly overcame such an obstacle – they considered it just a matter of fun and excitement. Juana's horse, Tiny, was still lame and she had to ride another horse which Harry had bought for £140 (a huge sum in those days). During the march the horse slipped and fell on Juana, breaking a bone in her foot. Horrified at the prospect of being separated from her Enrique, she demanded a mule and a Spanish lady's saddle. Officers combed the town for a suitable mule and for a well-cushioned saddle, and the problem was quickly resolved. The march continued and on 7 June 1813, from early morning until past six in the evening the whole army passed though Palencia – cavalry, artillery, infantry and baggage in a never-ending stream. At the end of the day's march, many eager hands helped Juana descend from her quaint saddle.

As the Allies advanced, they once again approached Burgos where the Light Division, eager to fight the French in open country, hated the thought of a siege there, with the grim reminder from Badajoz of the number of their comrades killed on the bastions, embrasures, curtain walls and other defences – 'and we wished Burgos to the devil'. Then, to their delight, there were several terrific explosions, and they realized that the French 'had blown Burgos to where we wished it', and then retreated.

To Harry's relief Juana's foot soon got better. His main concern at the prospect of leaving her behind was that the local people would punish her for being married to a heretic. Many other soldiers observed that they were welcomed by the locals when they drove out the French, but were still regarded as heretics.

As the Division approached Vitoria, on 18 June 1813, Harry looked back on a wonderful march, with the whole army in great fighting order, 'with every man in better wind than a trained pugilist'. At the Battle of Vitoria, Wellington commanded about 70,000 men, including substantial numbers of Portuguese and Spanish regulars. The battle took place just west of the town and at midday a local peasant, trained by the remarkably effective Spanish guerrillas, informed Wellington that a key bridge over the River Zadorra was unguarded. Once again at the centre of action, he immediately gave orders for a brigade of the Light Division under Kempt – who had been wounded at Badajoz – to advance swiftly over the bridge. This action played a key role in the defeat of the French. In the middle of the battle Harry, renowned for his confidence and initiative, had been sent to Dalhousie, the notoriously hesitant commander of the 7th Division. When he rushed up to the General, asking for orders for the brigade of the Light Division which was temporarily under his command, Harry heard him say, 'Take the village.' Knowing Dalhousie's timidity, Harry deliberately misunderstood the order, galloped off, ignoring cries to come back, and passed the order to attack. Instantly, swarms of riflemen, keeping up a rate of fire none could resist, rushed at the village, drove out the French and captured twelve guns. Afterwards, Harry recorded the great pride he felt for his riflemen: 'beautiful shots and undaunted as bulldogs'. Their loyalty and skill in supporting each other had defeated the French.

The brief and critical action of the Light Division – assisted by Harry's deliberate misunderstanding – broke the initial French defences, and then the tough and aggressive Picton, leading the 3rd

Division, drove through the gap ahead of the dilatory Dalhousie. While heavy fighting continued in the centre, Portuguese and Spanish units fought fiercely on the left flank, drove in the French defences and cut the road to Pamplona.

Wellington's decisive victory at Vitoria ended any major organized resistance by the French under King Joseph and Marshal Jourdan, although some very stiff fights still remained at Pamplona and San Sebastian. The victory also brought a fabulous amount of booty, looted by the French after six years of occupation. Jourdan even lost his marshal's baton, which Wellington sent off to the Prince Regent – who returned the compliment and promoted Wellington to Field Marshal. The French soldiers fled from the field of Vitoria, but in addition there were large numbers of French civilians, mostly in carriages loaded with loot, who abandoned everything and fled for their lives. After Vitoria, the temptations of massive booty led to a serious breakdown in discipline. The troops looted crates and crates of wine and brandy, Renaissance pictures, jewellery, gold regalia and fine clothes from King Joseph's entourage. The 14th Light Dragoons (later the King's Royal Hussars) captured his solid silver chamber pot, a valuable artefact that is still treasured in the Regiment and is filled with champagne for toasts on dinner nights in the Officers' Mess. Nearly all the troops were weighed down with legs of mutton and sausages, and many were too drunk to march – even Wellington, who was fuming with anger, could not get them to move off. His dispatch to Earl Bathurst in Whitehall grimly admitted that the troops had pocketed a million pounds sterling. By sheer chance, the whole of the French army's pay had arrived in Vitoria just before the battle, only a fraction of which subsequently reached Wellington's war chest!

During the Vitoria battle, Harry was getting on his horse to observe the action from a gun battery when the horse collapsed and lay as if dead. He managed to jump off and quickly looked for the wound. Finding none he gave the horse a sharp kick in the nose and to his surprise it jumped up unharmed. The gunners assured him its collapse was caused by the explosion from the cannon fire. In the meantime, rumours that Harry had been killed spread quickly and reached Juana, who was distraught. When he galloped up and assured her he was neither wounded nor dead, she collapsed in an ecstasy of joy.

That evening they found shelter in a large barn and in the morning, as they were getting ready to move off, Juana thought she heard some moaning from the hayloft above the barn. Harry climbed up and found that there were about twenty French officers, all severely wounded, and one, tended by a woman, close to death. All over Spain, French reprisals on the Spanish population had been brutal and savage, and the officers clearly expected to have their throats cut. To their surprise Harry's Headquarters gave them what help they could and even provided some water and breakfast. The woman, who was Spanish, had a little thoroughbred pug dog and she begged Juana to accept it in return for their kindness. At first Harry was aghast at the idea, but Juana convinced him. They called it Vitoria, or Vitty, and for several years – even up to Waterloo – it became a favourite of the Division as 'the most sensible little brute nature ever produced'.

The kindness Harry and Juana showed to the French officers was in stark contrast to the devastation the army encountered as it pursued the enemy. They found villages in flames, and corpses of men, women and children strewn about unburied. Harry said that the seat of war was hell upon earth, even when stripped of the atrocities committed by the French. He added that if the people at home had seen a twentieth part of the horrors that he had, they would grumble less at the war taxes 'and the pinching saddle of the national debt'.

One evening during the advance, a stout Frenchman approached Harry's position, saying he wanted to see the Duke. He was immediately taken to General Vandeleur. Although a thoroughly unpleasant and distasteful man, courtesy dictated that he dine with them. They initially thought he was a spy; he later told General Vandeleur that he was indeed and, moreover, was in the service of the Duke. He could not leave that night, as they did not know, specifically, where the Duke's Headquarters was, and the night was pitch black anyway; so the Frenchman, whom Harry clearly despised, was given to him to look after. They subsequently heard it was in fact true and the man was of great use to the Duke, having been in King Joseph's household.

The next day Harry's Light Division bypassed Pamplona and was cantoned in the village of Offala. However, it was necessary to establish observation posts to cover Pamplona, and General Vandeleur and Harry rode out to reconnoitre suitable positions. They had a very athletic and active guide with them who was overtalkative and full of the battle of Vitoria. When he asked the General's name, Harry told him, then heard him muttering the name over to himself several times before running up to the General and entering into conversation. The General quickly called Harry over to him, for he could not speak a word of Spanish. 'What's the fellow say?' 'He is telling all he heard from the Frenchmen who were billeted in his house in the retreat. He is full of anecdote.' The Spaniard then looked Vandeleur full in the face and said, 'Yes, they say the English fought well, but had it not been for one General Bandelo, the French would have gained the day.' 'How the devil did this fellow know?' said Vandeleur, secretly rather pleased. Harry did not tell the General anything different, so he happily thought his Brigade being sent to assist the 7th Division was the cause of the Frenchmen's remark. The guide, just like a 'cute Irishman or American', gave Harry a knowing wink.

There was a more sinister follow-up to this incident. Harry and Juana were billeted in this man's house. Before dinner he invited Harry to go down and see his cellar of fine wine. He guided Harry down narrow stone steps, opened a door, and with a maniacal cry pointed to four bodies lying on the floor, grunting, 'There lie four of the devils who thought to subjugate Spain.' Harry realized he was alone in a dark, narrow cellar with a homicidal maniac, and his instinct of self-preservation prompted him to admire the deed. He added, 'My blood was frozen, to see the noble science of war and the honour and chivalry of arms reduced to the practices of midnight assassins.' Continuing to humour the man, Harry asked how he had overpowered four strong-looking soldiers. The maniac laughed and explained that he had invited them down to the cellar, plied them with wine until they collapsed in a drunken stupor, then killed them with his stiletto, which he was again holding in his hand. When Harry returned from the cellar, Juana thought he looked a bit pale, but he did not explain.

In contrast to the horrors of that night, the next day, a Sunday, they reached a beautiful small town after a short march, and in the afternoon, affected by the peace and serenity of the place, Harry reminisced about the Sundays of his youth in Whittlesey: 'The very pew in church, the old peasants in the aisle; the friendly neighbours' happy faces ... in short, the joys of home, for amidst the eventful scenes of such a life, recollection will bring the past in view and compare the blessings of peace with the cruel horror of war!' Juana noticed his pensiveness, but he felt he could not mention home because of the trauma she had suffered in her home in Badajoz.

The army quickly adapted from the horrors of battle to the relative calm of a victorious advance. The irrepressible Johnny Kincaid, who fell in love with remarkable frequency but remained a bachelor all his life, described the social life when their units occupied a pleasant town, in his book *Adventures in the Rifle Brigade*. For their 'usual evening dances' officers collected as many women as possible, 'whether countesses or sextonesses', and entertained them generously with food and drink. On one such occasion, in a masked ball, Juana thought that Harry was flirting with a Spanish woman, so she went over and boxed his ears. They both had fiery tempers and Harry, enraged, called Juana a fiery little varmint. This led to a monumental row, but like all their rows, ended up with tears, kisses and passionate embraces.

Soldiers in every age know how dramatically the change of a commander can affect their lives. In the campaign up to Vitoria, General Vandeleur had commanded the Brigade of the Light Division. He was liked and respected as a sound military leader, who was careful with the lives of his men. Both officers and men were sorry when he was posted off to command a cavalry brigade. Harry and Juana were particularly upset because they enjoyed a delightful and relaxed relationship with him, and they frequently shared his accommodation and ate together. Harry was thunderstruck when General Skerrett, who succeeded Vandeleur, made it clear that Harry was only to go to the General's quarters when asked. As the Division advanced towards the Pyrenees, Harry and his colleagues became more and more concerned because Skerrett, whom Harry considered 'a bilious fellow', appeared ignorant of the true role both of the Greenjackets and of the Light Division. At the same time as the unfortunate change, Napoleon recalled Marshal Soult to command the remaining French forces in northern Spain, and where necessary to overrule the weak and vacillating King Joseph, Napoleon's brother.

Soult, known to the British as 'Old Salt', the ablest French commander in Spain, quickly restored morale in his forces as they withdrew and fought many effective defensive actions in the foothills of the Pyrenees.

A hard-fought action near the small town of Vera – about 10 miles from the French border and halfway between Pamplona and San Sebastian – highlighted the increasing French resistance and Skerrett's incompetence. Skerrett had orders to cut off the retreat of a French division at a bridge over a deep gorge. Harry, usually in the front line of swiftly moving action in order to make sound reconnaissances and tactical assessments, had always found that Vandeleur welcomed his advice. Near the bridge over the swollen river was a group of houses held by a company of the Rifles commanded by Harry's colleague, Daniel Cadoux. Harry realized that the French were about to attack. He rushed up to Skerrett and suggested, urgently, that another battalion be sent to support Cadoux. Skerrett replied haughtily, 'Is that your opinion?' and refused to give the order. Increasing French attacks quickly captured the houses and the bridge, and inflicted heavy casualties on the defenders. However, it was impossible for the French to hold the position unless they counter-attacked the British overlooking the houses. Characteristically, Harry said to Skerrett, 'You see now what you have permitted, General, and we must retake these houses, which we ought never to have lost.' He accepted this and said, 'I believe you are right.' Harry could take it no longer and galloped up to Colonel Colborne, in command of the 52nd, who was as angry as Harry. 'Oh, sir, it is melancholy to see this. General Skerrett will do nothing; we must retake those houses. I told him what would happen.' 'I am glad of it, for I was [as] angry [as] you.' The houses were relatively easily retaken when the enemy realized that in the face of determined assaults, they were unable to maintain their defensive position which was overlooked from the high ground. Although Harry was pretty scathing about him, interestingly, Colonel Bunbury in *Reminiscences of a Veteran*, writes: 'Skerrett as an individual was brave to rashness; but I should have doubted it had I not so frequently witnessed proofs of his cool intrepidity and contempt of danger. At the head of troops, he was the most undecided, timid, and vacillating creature I ever met with.'

The river was now very swollen after torrential rain, making it unfordable anywhere else, and the guarding of the bridge therefore even more vital. Harry suggested the whole of the 2nd Battalion Rifle Brigade should be positioned in the houses, the bridge should be barricaded and the 52nd should be in close support. Skerrett laughed and, ordering the whole Battalion into position, said, 'You may leave a picquet of one officer and thirty men at the bridge.' Harry had a little memo pad in his pocket and took it out, for the first time ever, to note the General's orders. He read what he had written and asked if that was his order. Skerret said, 'Yes, I have already told you so.' Harry, somewhat insolently replied, 'We shall repent this before daylight.' But the General was impervious to reason. Upon which Harry galloped down to the houses, ordered the Battalion to retire and told his brother Tom, the Adjutant, to assemble a force of an officer and thirty men to defend the bridge. They all thought he was mad. Tom said, 'Cadoux's company is for picquet.' Cadoux rode up and could scarcely believe what he heard, then began to criticize Harry for not supporting them in the morning. Harry replied, 'Scold away, all true; but no fault of *mine*. But come, no time for jaw, the picquet!' Cadoux said, 'My company is so reduced this morning, I will stay with it if I may. There are about fifty men.' Harry promptly agreed, for he had much time for Cadoux's ability and courage, and told him he was likely to be attacked an hour or two before daylight. Cadoux agreed, 'Most certainly I shall, and I will now strengthen myself, and block up the bridge as well as I can, and I will, if possible, hold the bridge until supported; so, when the attack commences, instantly send the whole Battalion to me, and, please God, I will keep the bridge.' As darkness fell, Harry rode as fast as he could to tell Colborne, in whom he had complete faith and confidence. Having read Harry's memo he agreed that, as soon as the attack commenced, his Battalion should move down the heights on the flank of the 2nd Battalion of the 95th, which would advance to support Cadoux. They parted with Harry in deep foreboding as to what was going to happen.

In the course of the night, intelligence was received that the enemy were attempting to withdraw over the swollen river. It was therefore highly likely that they would try to capture the bridge before daylight. As Skerret and Harry were discussing it, noise of the attack began with shouts of 'En avant, en avant! L'Empereur récompensera le premier qu'avancera', and Cadoux's retaliatory fire could be heard. The only hope was that Cadoux could hold the bridge until reinforced. The fire of the enemy was extreme as they put in desperate and determined assaults. On three successive occasions, with half his intrepid force, Cadoux charged and drove the enemy back over the bridge, the other half remaining in the houses to give supporting fire. His hope and confidence that he would be reinforced sustained him until he was eventually shot in the head. At this critical moment his Company was driven back; the French column and rearguard crossed and, by keeping near the bed of the river, succeeded in escaping, although the riflemen came to the support of Cadoux's men with as much speed as distance allowed, and by daylight, Colborne was where he promised.

Harry was soon at the bridge. It was a scene of indescribable carnage. The bridge was almost choked with the dead; the enemy's losses were enormous, many of their men having drowned, and all their guns were left in the river a mile or two below the bridge. The number of dead was so great that the bodies were thrown into the river in the hope that the current would carry them downstream, but the many rocks impeded them and when the river subsided soon after, the stench was terrible.

Cadoux, whom Harry respected as a brave and able officer, lay dead among the corpses of his riflemen. After a bitter and angry exchange, Skerrett admitted his mistake, but Harry never forgave him for his arrogant stubbornness which caused the debacle and the unnecessary loss of life. He added, 'our gallant fellows were knocked over by a stupidity heretofore not exemplified.'

Although Harry spent his career campaigning, and took part in many hard-fought and bloody actions, the loss of Cadoux affected him deeply. He wrote at length, explaining that at first he did not like Cadoux who appeared to be snooty and aloof, but after taking part in several actions together, gained a deep respect for his bravery and professionalism. Harry wrote in his autobiography: 'I wept over his gallant remains with a bursting heart.'

Wellington felt extremely annoyed at the failure to cut off the French division at the bridge but 'as was his rule he never said anything when disaster could not be amended'. He kept tight control over the brisk actions and rapid marches along the front between San Sebastian, where supplies and reinforcements for the Allies were unloaded, and the pass of Roncevalles through the Pyrenees. In his description of these actions, which included grim marches up precipitous mountain slopes, and men were lost over vertical cliffs, Harry still seemed obsessed with his loathing of Skerrett. With obvious glee, he told the story of how Skerrett, already notorious for his meanness, decided to give a dinner, and asked Harry if he could obtain wine and mutton. Through his ever-ready contacts Harry acquired eight sheep and a dozen bottles of claret, and was dumbfounded when Skerrett replied that he only wanted one sheep and two bottles of wine. Harry then told the story how the wine ran out before the meal had started and Skerrett became a laughing stock. The story quickly circulated through the Brigade.

To Harry's delight, Skerrett was soon replaced by Colonel Colborne, an officer brought up in the best tradition of the Light Infantry, with links to Sir John Moore himself, and who was to become a life-long friend. The Light Division had complete confidence in Colborne as an able and conscientious leader, who had a good eye for ground, anticipated the enemy's moves, and was cool and collected under fire. In October 1813, the Division, with Harry's unit in the lead, advanced towards the pass of Vera. Still a Captain, Harry went with Colborne to reconnoitre the French defences on the heights. Colborne said that if they took the French position, 'If you are not knocked over you shall be a brevet-major in the morning.' The proposal to promote Harry over the heads of more senior captains in the Brigade was controversial and had to be resolved by Wellington himself. He agreed to Harry's promotion, on condition he went to another brigade, but Harry remained loyal to his Brigade, and especially to Colborne whom he admired, so he refused the promotion. In another hard-fought action, when Juana was sheltering in a cottage near the front line, she saw a horse similar to Harry's gallop past, dragging a lifeless body in the stirrup. Frantic with fear, she rushed after the horse and when she saw it was not Harry's she collapsed in a wave of emotion and relief. Harry, as usual, was unharmed.

Brisk actions continued in the hills and ravines of the Pyrenees. In a situation of rapid movement, Colborne and Harry, aware of the need for accurate reconnaissance, sometimes found themselves ahead of their own troops. On one occasion, they suddenly confronted a French column in a ravine. Colborne, alert to their danger and 'with the bearing of a man supported by 10,000', rushed up to the French officer and said, 'You are cut off. Lay down your arms.' The officer accepted Colborne's threat, ordered his men to lay down their arms, and presented his sword to Colborne, who quickly ordered the French to turn left and march away from their weapons. He turned to Harry and grinned, whispering to him to gather some men as swiftly as possible in case the French realized they had been duped. Colborne and Harry, with less than fifty men, had captured a French unit of twenty officers and 400 men. Illustrating the chivalry of the time, Colborne later returned the sword to the French officer, saying he could wear it with pride.

Soon after the Allies crossed the border into France, a minor incident illustrated Wellington's total control. He met a subaltern from Colborne's brigade escorting some prisoners. The young officer said he knew they were in France because they had got hold of pigs and poultry, which they could not get in Spain. Wellington's rule, established during his campaigns in India, was at all costs not to antagonize the local population. He therefore summoned Colborne, gave him a mild rebuke and added, 'Stop it in future, Colborne.'

Having captured the heights of Vera, the Light Division established their general hospital nearby. As Harry was going to the hospital to visit the wounded, he passed a desperately wounded French soldier, who cried out for help. Harry went off and arranged for a stretcher party to fetch the poor man and take him to hospital. Some weeks later, when he was involved in a parley and the exchange of prisoners, a voluble French prisoner shouted out that Harry had saved his life. Harry wrote: 'I never saw gratitude so forcibly expressed in my life.'

Soult's effective leadership meant that the Light Division faced stiff resistance as they grimly pressed forward through the Pyrenees and into the plains of south-west France. In one brilliant and successful action against the French, Harry's horse was shot and before he could jump clear it rolled on him and covered him in blood. When she saw him Juana was horrified, but once again, her worst fears were not realized. She had clearly won the affection of both officers and men in the Division and on one occasion Colonel Gilmour, who commanded a battalion of the

Rifles, offered her the comfort of a hut, made largely of mud, which had been built for him, but which he was leaving. When Harry returned, all was warm and snug, and a meal prepared. Soon after they 'had retired to our nuptial couch', a violent storm of rain blew up, the roof collapsed and left both covered in black mud. Juana 'laughed herself warm'.

During the late summer and autumn of 1813, although there were fierce clashes, with both sides sustaining casualties, there was little animosity between the British and French armies outside of battle, and often picquets were placed by mutual agreement. Because Spain had suffered appalling atrocities at the hands of the French occupiers, the same could not be said of the Spanish as they advanced into France. Wellington kept very tight control over Spanish units, knowing they might seek revenge, and he was determined that the local French people should not be antagonized. He dealt severely with cases of theft, even hanging some thieves as an example. Napoleon wanted the people to rise up against the invaders, but Wellington effectively made sure that this did not happen.

When the Light Division was leading the advance, Wellington would often be in their Headquarters, discussing tactics, both for the Division and down to battalion level. He took part in a discussion about a Light Division attack on La Petite Rhune, in which both Colborne and Harry were involved. They led a secret night advance and then made a dawn attack which took the French completely by surprise. Harry described the attack, which is mentioned in Napier's *History of the War in the Peninsula*, as 'the most beautiful attack ever made'. Despite this success they suffered further casualties as they advanced. Kincaid described how Colonel Colborne was shot through the lungs, but was saved by prompt medical attention.

By the end of November 1813, the Allies were firmly established in France, and were fighting in the area between Nivelle and Bayonne on the French Atlantic coast. During some desultory skirmishing and in a dispute over the position of some French picquets, Harry ordered his men to fire a few rounds over the heads of the French defences. He commented that he was reluctant to shoot any man in a cold-blooded manner – as if war was some macabre game to be played according to strict rules of decency and etiquette.

Early in December, at a time when Harry was physically exhausted, he had a vivid and disturbing dream that the enemy were attacking his father's house in Whittlesey, and his mother was in danger. He woke suddenly from the dream and shouted, 'Stand to your arms.' This woke Colborne who was sleeping nearby and Harry apologized, explaining that he had just had a nightmare. He was deeply upset over this dream and noted the exact time in his diary. Some days later, he received a letter from his father saying his mother had died at the very time of his dream – the letter and the diary entry still exist. In his autobiography, he then indulges in a highly emotional and sentimental tribute to his mother, recalling the moving moment when he first went off to the war. His ten siblings were weeping as his mother embraced him saying, 'Remember you are born a true Englishman.' During a long period of depression which Harry suffered after the loss of his mother, Juana helped to restore his spirits, and reminded him that she had lost all her family and her home. She said tenderly, 'I live alone for you – my all, my home, my kindred.'

The Light Division spent a relatively static time over Christmas 1813 in the area of Bayonne, where food and good Bordeaux wine were plentiful. When not actually fighting there was often serious professional rivalry between the divisions, and at Bayonne the powerful and aggressive Picton, commanding the 3rd Division, who had been wounded at Badajoz and who was always bitterly critical of the Light Division, had a severe clash with Colonel Barnard. The Duke, conscious of the fierce characters among his officers, soon calmed the dispute.

During the advance near Bayonne, Harry and Juana had stayed the night in the house of a poor French widow, who had shown Juana a valuable Sèvres bowl. The next day they had a very long rough ride and slept in a roadside cottage. In the morning, to their amazement, their servant brought in their goat's milk in the Sèvres bowl. He was roundly rebuked, but explained that he thought the bowl would be ideal for serving their milk. Soon after breakfast Juana told Harry that she had to visit a wounded officer, but instead she got hold of West, their trusty groom, and galloped off to return the bowl to the widow. In the evening, having ridden over 30 miles through dangerous territory patrolled by the

French, she returned, late for dinner, and explained what she had done. Colonel Barnard was delighted and said she was a true heroine.

As the fighting drew to an end, Harry reminisced about the fine characters with whom he had shared the campaign – Johnny Kincaid, Charlie Beckwith, John Colborne, later a field marshal, Bill Beresford who as a Viscount enjoyed a long and distinguished military and political career, and Edward Pakenham, Harry's close friend who was to be killed in the attack on New Orleans. Harry's subsequent career, always accompanied by Juana, took him to Africa and India, and he frequently met his old friends and hardened veterans of the Peninsula. As he looked back he proudly described the excellence of 'his Riflemen', so well trained, such accurate shots, and so effective in skirmishing ahead of the main body of troops. After one bloody clash with the French he recorded that he never saw the dead lie so thick, except later at Waterloo. The Duke himself said, 'I require no proof of the destructive power of your Rifles.'

By March 1814, although the campaign was nearly over, Wellington was still directing four divisions – the 3rd, the 4th, the 6th and the Light Division, and then on 10 April, the army prepared for a final showdown at Toulouse. This proved to be a grim and hard-fought battle with heavy casualties on both sides, with Wellington directing the divisions on the ground. The very next day, news came that the war was over and Napoleon had abdicated. The Allies, including the Spanish units which had fought valiantly at Toulouse, occupied the city. Harry, Juana and their friends were allocated a delightful furnished chateau complete with a French cook. 'We were as wanton and extravagant as lawless sailors just landed from a long voyage. The feeling of no war, no picquets, no alerts, no apprehension of being turned out, was so novel after six years of perpetual and vigilant war, it is impossible to describe the sensation.'

In Toulouse, a formal funeral service took place in the Protestant church for a colonel killed in the final battle, and was attended by most of the officers including the Duke. The service made a huge impact on Harry, bringing back for him memories of all those gallant soldiers and friends left on the fields of Spain, buried with some trifling ceremony or none at all. He had witnessed, in the badly wounded, the anguish of dying alone in a foreign land.

The Royalist city of Toulouse seems to have welcomed the British divisions and the end of wartime privations. The officers enjoyed a vivacious social life of theatres, balls and fêtes with an abundance of food and drink, and 'the indolence of repose after the excitement of a relentless and cruel war'. Harry rejoiced in the celebrations with Juana who had shared uncomplainingly all the hardships and suffering of the campaign from Badajoz onwards. He noted too that the soldiers also had a happy time because the local area, like most of France, had been denuded of men by the endless demands of Napoleon's armies. Generous local provision was a boon for the British because officers and soldiers alike were nine months in arrears of pay. Near their billets there were some 'Napoleonist' units who were 'brutally sulky and uncivil', but Harry and Juana ignored them, revelled in the joys of peace in a lush and prosperous countryside and celebrated the first momentous year of their marriage.

During their brief time in Toulouse enjoying the benefits of peace, the British received a kind welcome into people's homes, and as Kincaid said, 'made love to the pretty girls with which the place abounded'. The officers continued to organize dances but on one occasion, during Lent, the ladies wondered whether they should attend. However, 'they arranged things with their conscience and joined in the waltz right merrily'.

There were tears when the order came to move to Bordeaux, with many expressions of genuine affection, and a year later, after Waterloo, the units received many letters expressing concern about casualties. Near the Biscay coast the troops found plentiful supplies of fresh eggs, butter and, above all, fresh fish, but at Saint Jean de Luz 'the prices were absolutely suicidal'. Kincaid observed that by the sea the women had unrivalled complexions and wore lots of yellow petticoats, but behind the joyous and light-hearted celebrations of peace and plenty lay the sombre thought, yet to be solved, of what was there for soldiers to do in peacetime. The Government was going to have not only discharged and unemployed soldiers on its hands, but also many *unemployable* due to severe wounds, both physical and mental. There was little provision for either and the land was soon to see sad knots of ex-soldiers begging in the streets or being turned over to the poorhouse. Trouble was being stored up for the future. This, of course, was the same for the French and it was therefore no wonder that former soldiers flocked to Napoleon's Colours on his escape from Elba. Harry was a highly experienced combat officer but he had never done anything else. Was it to be peacetime soldiering, with little foreseeable action, or pastures new? For Harry and Juana, what did the future hold?

# Chapter 4

## America
## April 1814 to March 1815

Harry and Juana need not have worried: in April, Harry was sent for by Colonel Colborne, his much-admired Commanding Officer, badly wounded in the arm at Ciudad Rodrigo, who told him he was unlucky, despite his considerable combat experience, not to have been promoted to major. He must now, he said, leave for America, to which a large force was being sent, and he, Colborne, would see to it that he would be appointed Brigade Major. While now there was no question of promotion by purchase, there is no doubt that Harry's name was well known in the military hierarchy, and he had a number of powerful and influential friends, such as General Sir Edward Pakenham, Wellington's brother-in-law, and, specifically, General Ross, who was to command the American expeditionary force. Thus Harry was appointed Deputy Adjutant General (a senior administrative staff officer) on Ross's staff in the rank of major.

The departure from Toulouse in May brought many moments of intense emotion. For Harry and Juana, the black cloud of their impending separation, while Harry went off to take part in the expedition to America, hung over everything else. Harry had landed in the Peninsula with the Battalion about a thousand strong, but now only about half that number were able to parade. Harry's reputation as the best Brigade Major in the Light Division, his frenetic energy and his caring leadership were rewarded when the whole Battalion lined up to cheer him farewell. This, too, was an overwhelmingly emotional moment, as they cheered their 'Mr Smith' and begged him to come back. As he left, he and they remembered, as all units do who have fought tough battles, the friends and comrades who have been killed or wounded and left along the way.

Harry was torn between his future career prospects and remaining with his beautiful wife. The war with Napoleon was effectively over but there remained significant conflicts in other parts of the world, notably in America in what was termed the War of 1812. So, was Harry to languish in peacetime soldiering, with little money and unlikely advancement, but with his wife, or take on further adventures, temporarily, without her? A dilemma a modern soldier thoroughly understands.

The tension between the United States and Great Britain arose over two main issues: the British claim to the right of search on the high seas of neutral vessels suspected of carrying contraband or strategic materials to France and her allies; and American ambitions to assimilate those parts of Canada adjacent to the Great Lakes and the St Lawrence River.

One can imagine the anguished discussions over their future separation and Juana's life without him. Harry wrote:

> I knew I must leave behind my young, fond and devoted wife, my heart was ready to burst, and all my visions for our mutual happiness were banished in search of the bubble reputation. I shall never forget her frenzied grief when, with a sort of despair, I imparted the inevitable separation that we were doomed to suffer, after all our escapes, fatigue, and privation; but a sense of duty surmounted all these domestic feelings.

Harry and Juana travelled by boat down the Garonne, together with his brother Tom, still nursing a wounded knee, and the tough but diminutive Bob Digby, a close colleague and friend. Digby had an old and reliable servant who was going to accompany Juana to England, because West, Harry's servant, was going to America with him. During several days' leisurely travel, the party stopped at riverside inns, which they found to be much cleaner and more comfortable than many they had known in Spain. When they arrived in Bordeaux, Harry insisted that they put up in the best hotel, and they enjoyed a few days of luxury and pleasure in the prosperous and attractive port city lying along the estuary. When the actual moment of parting arrived, Juana said, 'I lose the only thing my life hangs on.' Such was the intensity of their love for each other that Harry was nearly overcome with emotion and Juana actually fainted. Digby took charge, told Harry to be on his way and promised to look after Juana. He and Tom arranged for her passage on the next ship for England, together with Tiny, her favourite horse, and dogs and greyhounds.

Juana, oppressed by her separation from Harry, had a dull but uneventful voyage from Bordeaux to Portsmouth, though there were on the ship several good friends from the Light Bobs, who had taken part in the campaign from Badajoz onwards. With their respect and affection for Harry and Juana, they did their best to lift her spirits. She stayed briefly in Portsmouth, while Tom arranged for the horses and dogs to be taken on to Whittlesey, and when that was done he hired a post-chaise to take them to London.

Tom, excited at being back in England, eagerly pointed out all the interesting places on the London road as they passed the Hog's Back and Guildford, and then saw the Thames. Juana, who had briefly seen the fashions in Bordeaux and Portsmouth, was relieved when Tom said that he was rather short of money and suggested that, initially, they stayed in a modest inn. When he apologized for this, she just laughed and reminded him of the tumbledown and bug-infested places they had often occupied in Spain.

Having lived in Badajoz and having stayed briefly in Madrid, Juana was overwhelmed by the bustle and the traffic in central London. It appeared to be a most prosperous city, and she found the shops in Bond Street and Oxford Street quite intimidating. Tom was a model of decorum and concern, but Juana, as she had with the other young officers in the Rifles, teased him unmercifully about his various lady friends in Spain and France, but promised she would not tell the family. She was acutely aware that she had learnt very little English and found it very difficult to communicate at all with English people. She was therefore greatly relieved when they found rooms for her in Panton Square near the Haymarket, with a French woman, Madame Dupont.

As soon as Juana was installed in Madame Dupont's very respectable house, Tom raised the question of visiting the family in Whittlesey, but she, very conscious of her lack of English, was extremely apprehensive about meeting such a large and, as she saw it, formidable group. Little did she know that they were just as concerned at the prospect of meeting her. She was determined to work hard at learning English, and then she would be able to meet the large family when Harry returned from America. So while Tom went off to see the family, Juana was left, lonely, isolated and love-lorn in central London. Her landlady had arranged for her to have lessons with a rather prim spinster, who was accustomed to teaching well-brought-up young ladies. She found Juana alarmingly unconventional and when she came out with some fruity phrases which she had picked up from the Riflemen during the campaign, her teacher was horrified. Soon afterwards they found an elderly man who coached her in language and pronunciation, and enjoyed the humour of the situation.

Juana slowly explored London and even walked in Hyde Park, but found the elegant well-dressed ladies walking with their proud escorts to be very daunting, while all the time she was aching for her Enrique. She waited week after week for the one solace which could overcome her loneliness, a letter from Harry, yet it did not come, and she shared the anguish of all service wives whose loved ones are fighting in a far-off land.

Tom returned from his leave with the warm and loving family in Whittlesey, and tried to convince Juana that they were longing to see her. He had told them all about her and had tried to convince them that she was not a proud and formal Spanish matron. One sister who could speak French had written a letter of welcome, begging her to go and stay with them. Then Juana wanted to hear all about the horses and dogs. Harry's father was a fine horseman and had cared for them all, and Tom was able to reassure her that Tiny, who had carried her safely through so many adventures, was flourishing, but 'Old Chap', Harry's favourite horse, was old and sick and not likely to last long. The father had been amazed that Harry had allowed Juana to have such a spirited and difficult horse as Tiny.

She cheered up at the news of the horses and dogs now safely housed at Whittlesey, and became quite animated at the activities of so many old friends. She impressed her tutor with the casual way she referred to the Duke of Wellington, who had returned to London after another visit to Spain. After Tom's return from leave, it was arranged that his married sister, Mrs Alice Sargant, who lived near London, should come and visit Juana. A strong personality, who appeared daunting even to Harry, Mrs Sargant eventually came to visit but arrived unexpectedly, making Juana feel totally inadequate as she was not suitably dressed to receive visitors. At first Alice was amazed that the quiet, withdrawn and almost frightened-looking young girl could be Harry's wife. A rather tense and stilted conversation took place, during which Juana forgot even the little English she had so laboriously learnt. Alice kept asking questions in a somewhat imperious way, and received shorter and shorter answers. Both women felt increasingly embarrassed and conversation had nearly dried up when a servant announced two gentlemen. As Johnny Kincaid and George Simmons walked into the room the quiet, withdrawn girl leapt up and flung her arms around them with a babble of excited Spanish. The shock and joy of seeing two close friends was too much for Juana who then burst into tears. Kincaid gently chided her until gradually she calmed down and was able to introduce the two officers to her sister-in-law. Simmons then sat and chatted amiably with Alice, while Juana plied them with questions about other old friends, and above all for any news from America. Alice began to realize that her first impression had been wrong.

After the restrained first contact with the Smith family, Juana began to revive in the company of Johnny Kincaid and other friends from the Regiment who came to visit. They took her to Vauxhall Gardens, where there were fireworks displays, which enchanted her, and later Charlie Beckwith, a particularly close friend of Harry, arrived in London and took Juana to theatres and shows, trying to fill the gap until Harry returned. The kind thoughtfulness of friends from the Peninsula did relieve Juana's lonely tedium, but as the summer wore on their visits became fewer because they, like most people who could afford it, left London for pleasanter places by the sea, such as Brighton, or in the country, like Bath or Harrogate. The annual exodus from London took place because hot summer weather brought appalling stenches from piles of rubbish and ordure in the streets, with plagues of flies and wasps making life extremely unpleasant for everyone. For Juana, life seemed to stretch ahead as a lonely desert of boredom with no end in sight.

At last, in early September 1814, a letter arrived from Whittlesey, and it contained a letter from Harry. While this brought some relief, it really added to her apprehension. It had been sent off from Bermuda where Harry's ship had called in because of a severe storm, so he had not then even arrived in the war zone. While Harry assured her that she was in his thoughts both day and night and he was longing for their reunion, he did write amusingly about his interesting life on board, where he was deeply respected as a Peninsula veteran. He added colourful anecdotes about his fellow passengers and the ship's crew, but all this detail seemed to increase her lonely longing for her Enrique.

On leaving Juana in Bordeaux, Harry had handled his grief by leaping on his horse and riding hard for 20 miles towards his embarkation port, Paullic. He later wrote:

> I had a long ride before me on the noble mare destined to embark with me. On my way I reached a village where I received the attention of a kind old lady, who from her age had been exempt from having any troops quartered on her; but, the village being full of Rifle Brigade, Artillery, and Light Division fellows, the poor old lady was saddled with me. The Artillery readily took charge of my horse. The kind old grandmamma showed me into a neat little bedroom and left me. I threw myself on the bed as one *alone* in all the wide world, a feeling never before experienced, when my eye caught some prints on the wall. What should they be but pictures in representation of the *Sorrows of Werther*, and, strange though it be, they had the contrary effect upon me to that which at the first glance I anticipated. They roused me from my sort of lethargy of grief and inspired a hope which never after abandoned me. The good lady had a nice little supper of *côtelettes de mouton*, and the most beautiful strawberries I ever saw, and she opened a bottle of excellent wine. To gratify her I swallowed by force all I could, for her kindness was maternal.

After another long ride, Harry reached Paullic, and met up with his faithful soldier servant, West, who was devoted to Juana but, knowing how much it would upset Harry to speak of her, restrained himself from asking after his beloved mistress. West had found Harry a comfortable billet in the house of an elderly lady, of whom he wrote:

> One morning I heard a most extraordinary shout of joyful exclamation, so much so I ran into the room adjoining the one I was sitting in. The poor old woman says, 'Oh, come in and witness my happiness!' She was locked in the arms of a big, stout-looking, well-whiskered Frenchman. 'Here is my son, oh! my long-lost son, who has been a [prisoner] in England from the beginning of the war.' The poor fellow was a sous-officier in a man-of-war, and, having been taken early in the war off Boulogne, for years he had been in those accursed monsters of inhuman invention, 'the hulks', a prisoner. He made no complaint. He said England had no other place to keep their prisoners, that they were well fed by the English, but when, by an arrangement with France at her own request, the French Government fed them, they were half starved. The widow gave a great dinner-party at two o'clock, to which I was of course invited. The poor old lady said, 'Now let us drink some of this wine: it was made the year my poor son was taken prisoner. I vowed it should never be opened until he was restored to me, and this day I have broached the cask.' The wine was excellent. If all the wine-growers had sons taken prisoners, and kept it thus until their release, the world would be well supplied with good wine in place of bad. Poor family! It was delightful to witness their happiness, while I could but meditate on the contrast between it and my wretchedness. But I lived in hope.

When Harry embarked on the *Royal Oak*, he was very nervous of unwittingly breaching some Royal Navy etiquette, rules or conventions of behaviour, some of which survive to today (for instance, you are always *in* a ship but *on* a boat or yacht). Additionally, he was highly conscious that up to, and soon after, Trafalgar in 1805, the Royal Navy, headed by Nelson, was idolized by the people. However, since then, the

Army, with a series of astounding victories in the Peninsula under Wellington, had supplanted the Navy in the population's affections. Harry need not have worried; as a 'Peninsula' man, he was a hero enough in naval eyes. He received a warm welcome aboard by Admiral Malcolm and given a large glass of gin.

General Ross arrived the following morning and they set sail. The passage was uneventful until they encountered bad weather off Bermuda and lost their mizzen topmast. Harry, still morose from his separation from Juana, managed to send her a letter during a brief stop in port. They then sailed on from Bermuda, up the Chesapeake Bay, anchoring off the mouth of the Patuxent River. The senior commanders, including the aggressive Admirals Cochrane (this was not the other, even more famous, Admiral Sir Thomas Cochrane but Sir Alexander) and Cockburn, met aboard and decided to approach Washington up the Patuxent River in the frigates and smaller boats. Harry described progressing up this heavily forested river as a 'large fleet stalking through a wood'. Landing some 36 miles from Washington, Harry started to express some doubts about General Ross. He seemed to have assumed, with higher rank, an air of caution and timidity, and to lack the spirit that both Colonel Colborne and Harry remembered from his Peninsula days, so essential to fast-moving, opportunist operations which they now needed. The force, not in good order from their long time at sea, made contact with the enemy at Bladensburg on 24 August. To Harry's horror, Colonel Thornton, commanding the leading brigade, decided to attack immediately with no thought of reconnaissance or a possible diversion on the enemy's left flank further up the river. Harry suggested this, in his own inimitable way, to General Ross, who ignored him and allowed the attack to carry on. Having pointed out that the other two brigades could not come up in time to support the attack, Harry sardonically reported, 'It happened just as I said,' and the brigade was repulsed with heavy casualties. He was then ordered by Ross to bring up the other two brigades as fast as possible. Galloping on, without giving out any further detail, the General had two horses shot under him and was wounded in two or three places. Nevertheless, the battle was eventually won with British losses at about 300. Harry sourly remarked that

Colborne would have done the job with a mere forty or fifty casualties. On 26 August, the British marched the 5 miles into Washington, determined to sack it.

Washington, at the time a straggling village of some 8,000 inhabitants, was almost deserted. When a shot was fired from one of the first main houses which the British reached, killing Ross's horse, this was instantly revenged by setting the house on fire. After three or four volleys at the Capitol, the two detached wings were set on fire. The massive walls defied the flames, but all the interior was destroyed, with many valuable papers, including the Library of Congress – a piece of vandalism alleged to be in revenge for the burning of the Parliament House at York (now Toronto). The British went firm on Capitol Hill, but a detachment marched along Pennsylvania Avenue to the President's house in which the great hall had been converted into a military magazine. They set fire to the house and the offices of the Treasury and State Departments nearby; the next morning they destroyed the War Office and ransacked the office of National Intelligence. They burned the Arsenal, several private houses and some warehouses, but, in general, private property was respected. The only public building that escaped was the General Post Office and the Patent Office, both under the same roof, the burning of which was delayed by the entreaties of the superintendent. Its destruction was finally prevented by a tremendous tornado which passed over the city and for a while dispersed the British soldiers who sought refuge where they could, although several were buried in the ruins of falling buildings. The fiery Admiral Cochrane said, 'I am sorry you left a house standing in Washington – depend on it, it is a mistaken mercy.'

Flushed with success and urged on by the admirals, Ross decided to re-embark his men and do the same to Baltimore as he had done to Washington. Harry was appalled by the suggestion. The men, despite the effective walkover at Washington, were still in a pretty poor physical shape due to their long transatlantic voyage. Harry could see this, and urged Ross to rest them, allow time to replenish the force properly and get them fit. He also had severe doubts as to the advisability of attacking Baltimore for a number of strategic and tactical reasons. In order to reduce the enemy strength in Washington, Ross had indicated that his prime objective was Baltimore, thus a considerable force of American troops had been transferred there and were well positioned to defend the town. Secondly, Harry emphasized that *coup de main* operations, with a considerable element of surprise, work well once but the enemy would anticipate something of the sort a second time round, and so success was not likely to be so easy. The approach to Baltimore Harbour was bound to be effectively obstructed, although the Admirals confidently said they could clear any such obstruction in an hour. Harry doubted this and in the event was proved correct. Finally, Harry told Ross that his attack on Washington was a great success, but suggested that he should build on that, rather than taking the risk of losing at Baltimore and restoring the American confidence. Ross agreed but Harry, nevertheless, had a presentiment of looming disaster.

However, the dice were to roll again in his favour and, due to the sickness of Ross's ADC, Harry was ordered to take dispatches back to England. This was no ordinary mission. A bearer of such dispatches had to be a man of courage, resolve and integrity to meet every difficulty on the way with initiative and ingenuity. It was absolutely vital that the dispatches arrived safely and speedily and, not only that, the messenger had to be 'in his Commander's mind' so that he could answer the inevitable questions from the recipients of the dispatches, who, doubtless, would want to know more than just what they contained. They would wish to know what morale was like, how events were unfolding, what future intentions were and what demands were going to be made upon them. For Harry, of course, this was heaven. He was going to be reunited with his beloved Juana and return to England for the first time in seven years. So, aboard a fast frigate, Harry anchored off Spithead twenty-one days after leaving the United States.

During September 1814, although the weather was cooler, many of the summer smells still haunted the London streets. Juana continued her custom of rising early and taking a walk in the fresher morning air with Vitty, who had been her solace during her lonely vigil. On 22 September, she stepped out into Panton Square, walked a short distance and suddenly noticed a cab pull up. She gave a shriek of joy, 'Oh, Dios la mano de mi Enrique.' Harry described the moment:

Never shall I forget that shriek; never shall I forget the effusion of our gratitude to God, as we held each other in an embrace of love few can ever have known, cemented by every peculiarity of our union and the eventful scenes of our lives. Oh! You who enter into holy wedlock for the sake of connections – tame, cool, amiable, good, I admit – you cannot feel what we did. That moment of our lives was worth the whole of your apathetic ones for years. We were unbounded in love for each other, and in gratitude to God for his mercies.

Harry had landed at Portsmouth where, after a very brief stay at the George Inn while he arranged transport, he booked a chaise and four, and badgered his naval colleague to accompany him on a desperate rush to reach London. As the cab hurtled along, bumping and jarring over stretches of appalling roads, Harry explained that he was frantic to see his wife. He had left her four months before in Bordeaux and he did not know where she was, or if she was well, or even if she was still alive. His urgent pleas finally convinced his companion and the chaise hurried on. They reached Liphook and another argument took place, but after a hurried meal of bread, butter, cream and tea, they rushed on towards London. Harry wrote: 'The happy feeling of being in my native land once more, in health and in possession of every limb, excited a maddening sensation of doubt, anxiety and hope, all summed up in this – "Does your young wife live? Is she well?" Oh! The pain, the fear and the faith in Almighty God, who had so wonderfully protected me.'

They reached London at midnight, Harry delivered his crucial dispatches to Downing Street and then searched for rooms for the night for West and himself. They eventually found a hostelry open in Parliament Street but it only had one room. To the astonishment of the waiter and the chambermaid, Harry accepted it, hauled half the bedclothes onto the floor, 'according to our custom of seven years', and he and West settled down for a few hours sleep. Harry rose before dawn and hurried to the barracks to search for any colleague from the Rifles. To his delight, he found that Colonel Ross was there. To the horror of the orderly, Harry shouted, 'Stand to your arms,' Ross awoke and quickly embraced his old friend. He reassured Harry that Juana was indeed alive and well – he had seen her the previous afternoon. Harry wondered whether an excess of joy or grief was the most difficult to bear and burst into a flood of tears. He grabbed a hackney cab and in moments was in Panton Square.

After their ecstatic reunion – watched with some amusement by passers-by in the Square – Harry, all too soon, had to hurry off to see Lord Bathurst, the War Minister, who told him that the dispatches were so important that the Prince Regent wished to see him, and they rushed to Carlton House, the Prince's home. Here Harry was shown in to the most opulent room he had ever seen. Being unfamiliar with court etiquette, he became slightly nervous, but then remembered, 'I never quailed before the dear Duke of Wellington, with his piercing eye, nor will I now.' Bathurst, too, reassured him and told him to address the Prince as 'Sir', and not to turn his back on him. Harry quipped, 'Indeed, my profession is to show a good front.' He smiled to himself that here he was, Captain Smith from Whittlesey, sitting with the Prince Regent, while guns were firing from Parliament and the Tower to celebrate the news he had brought. He had taken with him a map of Washington, showing the buildings, including the White House, which had been destroyed. He sensed that the Prince disapproved of such a barbaric act. After a most affable interview, in which Harry had been amazed at the Prince's grasp of the detail of the war situation, they were shown out, and the Prince reminded Bathurst not to forget Harry's promotion.

After the interview, Bathurst invited Harry to dinner that night at his home in Putney – an invitation he could not refuse. Though he and Juana wanted to spend every moment together, she never demurred, and had already prepared his mess kit for any occasion. Having just returned from the war, Harry was the lion of the evening, and he was delighted to meet Lord Fitzroy Somerset with whom he had served from Badajoz to Toulouse. Harry was in high spirits and did not hesitate to give his opinion to the guests. He spoke enthusiastically of the Duke of Wellington as someone 'elevated above any human being', whereupon the elderly gentleman sitting next to him said, 'I am glad you approve of my brother.' Later, in conversation, Lord Fitzroy, who after Toulouse had travelled across Spain with the Duke, confirmed the Duke's opinion that the Light Division was the elite of the Army, and it sustained only half the losses of other divisions

The wife of General Ross, the commander who had sent Harry home with the dispatches, lived in Bath. Harry had promised to go and visit her as soon as possible, so he and Juana set off the following day. Their journey to Bath brought them complete and absolute joy. Stuck in London, Juana had seen almost nothing of the country, and she delighted in the beauty of the countryside and the rolling West Country hills. Mrs Ross welcomed them warmly in her home in Bath – little knowing that her husband had already been killed in America.

Before they had left for Bath, Harry had invited his father to come up to London to meet Juana, and when they returned to Panton Square, he had already arrived. They played a little trick on him, pretending that in her Spanish costume she was proud and stately, but she could not keep up the pretence for long and just flung herself into his arms, full of joy and delight. Harry was overjoyed at the instant warm friendship between his affectionate and kind-hearted father and Juana, who seemed to captivate everyone she met.

Soon afterwards they all left for Whittlesey, and Juana was warmly welcomed into a large and happy family. The father repeated his surprise that Juana had ridden Tiny because he had proved to be a very difficult horse to handle, but when she arrived at their home she went confidently to Tiny who obediently followed her into the house. She then mounted him and illustrated her relaxed and complete control. For nearly three weeks there was an outpouring of love and affection among the family – at having Harry back among them after so many years, and now with his sparkling young wife. The only brief shadow over their joy came when Harry and Juana went to see the tomb of his mother, the news of whose death had affected him so deeply during the last part of the Peninsula campaign. The tomb is still preserved in Whittlesey Church.

For three weeks – Harry's first home leave in seven years – he and Juana, on a wave of joy and emotion, spent every happy day visiting the numerous friends and relations of the Smith family; indeed, the whole of the small town of Whittlesey seemed to join in the celebrations. Juana captivated all the family with her charm, her sparkling personality and her quaint pronunciation of English. Her brothers and sisters-in-law delighted in this, and occasionally when their teasing went too far, she showed her fiery side and rounded on them with a torrent of Spanish, to the delight of her admiring husband.

This idyll could not last for ever and one day, when they returned from visiting his mother's grave, they found a letter from Horse Guards, which demanded instant action. The letter brought news of the death of General Ross and his replacement by Sir Edward Pakenham, who was to lead a new expedition to America, with Harry as Assistant Adjutant General – but still in the rank of major. To Harry, ever the professional soldier, this news brought the chance of action and promotion, but at the same time 'it once more raised that blighted word "separation" to be imparted to my faithful and adoring wife'. This time Juana would have the support of a large and loving family, and there was little time to mope. Within twenty-four hours, Harry, Juana and his father left for London with heavy hearts. Harry reported to Sir Edward Pakenham who told him that they were leaving from Portsmouth in a few days on the frigate *Statira*. 'Ned' Pakenham, Wellington's brother-in-law, was a man of great charm and much loved by his soldiers. His finest Peninsula hour had come at the Battle of Salamanca in 1812 when he had temporary command of the Third Division: responding swiftly to Wellington's order, 'Now's your time, Ned,' he manoeuvred his Division forward and broke the French centre, thus being instrumental in winning the battle, in an action that Wellington described as 'the most decisive and brilliant manoeuvre of the battle'. Wellington recorded his gratitude to Pakenham and his approval of him in a dispatch home, while at the same time alluding gently to one of his failings: 'Pakenham may not be the brightest genius.'

Harry met up with several Peninsula veterans and arranged to travel to Portsmouth with his old friend John Robb, now Inspector of Hospitals. They sent their baggage ahead with the ever faithful West. Then, with Juana in a state bordering on despair, and Harry, his heart fit to break, they parted and he hurried off to Portsmouth. They reached the George Inn at midnight and Harry – suffering an essentially modern problem – found that one of his portmanteaux had gone to Dover, and he had the dirty linen of some French officer. To his surprise, his errant luggage was eventually returned to him. When he left for Portsmouth, his father tenderly escorted Juana back to Whittlesey and to the warm embrace of a united and caring family, who did their best to comfort her during Harry's absence.

In America, after the sacking of Washington, Ross had given way to the fiery Admiral Cochrane and led an attack on Baltimore, despite Harry's earlier advice. This disastrous incident, which cost the British 300 casualties including Ross himself, virtually ended the campaign in that area, but further action took place in Alabama and around New Orleans, where the American defences were commanded by an able soldier, General Andrew Jackson.

General Pakenham, with Harry close at hand, landed in Louisiana on 25 December and moved close to New Orleans, having met up with Major General Keane, who had already had the worst of a preliminary skirmish with Jackson's men. Harry was with Pakenham on a reconnaissance very close to the enemy's lines when he saw some riflemen crouching down not more than a hundred yards away, and so he shouted, 'Ride away, Sir Edward, behind this bank, or you will be shot in a second. By your action you will be recognised as the Commander-in-Chief, and some riflemen are now going to fire.' Luckily, although good shots, the American riflemen were slow and the General was able to get away. Later that evening, Pakenham called for Harry and said, 'You gentlemen of the Craufurd school' (he was very fond of the Light Division) 'are very abrupt and peremptory in your manner to your Generals. Would you have spoken to Craufurd as you did to me to-day?' Harry said, 'Most certainly, for if I had not, and one of us had been killed or wounded, and he became aware I observed what I did when I spoke to you, he would have blown me up as I deserved. He taught us to do so.' Pakenham roared with laughter.

Jackson had prepared a good defensive position facing south-east, with the Mississippi River on his right and a cypress swamp on his left. Pakenham's plan to take him on was, in theory, a sound one. His men were to extend the Villere Canal by breaking through the levee along the riverbank so that it met the Mississippi. This would enable them to move by water all the way from the Bayou Bienvenu to the river. Under the cover of darkness, he anticipated a force of 1,500, under Colonel Thornton, could land on the west bank of the river and seize the American guns. This done, the guns could then be turned on the Americans from the flank and used to support the main assaulting force which would have moved forward, under cover of the morning fog.

However Thornton was frustrated by the slow process of loading equipment onto his shallow boats. After days of back-breaking labour, he had nevertheless assembled some forty of them in the new portion of the canal. Most of his men had had no sleep in the past few days and the cold and damp were starting to sap morale. Time was against them.

Only a short distance away, the Americans had been frantically working to fortify their positions along the north side of the Rodriguez Canal. Jackson had commandeered some 900 black slaves from local plantations to construct the massive earthen breastwork that ran 1,000 yards from the dense swampy forest to the banks of the Mississippi. A second line of defence was constructed a mile and a half back in case they needed to withdraw.

Anchored in the river to Jackson's right were the *Carolina* and the *Louisiana*, recently outfitted as ships of war. Both had been useful in keeping the British unsettled with sporadic fire over the previous few days. Cleverly anticipating a British attack on the batteries on the river's west bank, Jackson transferred cannon from the *Louisiana*, and an additional 400 militia under General David Morgan, to strengthen that position.

At 5.00am on 8 January, Pakenham moved up to the east bank of the Mississippi. Colonel Thornton's troops should have been across the river by now and closing on the American guns. Instead, most of his men were still waist-deep in mud, clearing away sections of the levee that had caved in on the canal passage and made it too shallow for the boats to cross. Only a few of the units were aboard and ready to move.

Pakenham, however, was insistent that the main force assaulted the American line before first light. He therefore ordered Thornton to proceed with the advance with what men he had. As they shoved off, it quickly became clear that the river was flowing faster than normal. They eventually made it across, but landed well below their target and lost even more precious time. Pakenham rode back to his headquarters through the fog and ordered his officers to make final preparations. There was considerable anxiety when they realized full well that Thornton had not yet successfully taken out the American guns. Nevertheless, they formed up, and with day about to break, hoped that Thornton would achieve his objective by the time they reached the

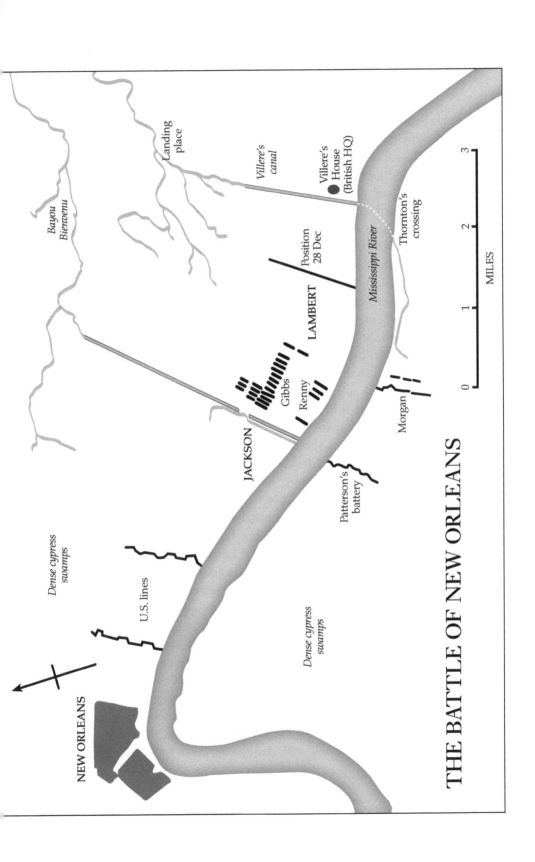

NEW ORLEANS

Dense cypress swamps

U.S. lines

Dense cypress swamps

Patterson's battery

JACKSON

LAMBERT

Gibbs

Renny

Morgan

Bayou Bienvenu

Landing place

Villere's canal

Position 28 Dec

Villere's House (British HQ)

Mississippi River

Thornton's crossing

0   1   2   3
MILES

# THE BATTLE OF NEW ORLEANS

American defences. As the morning mist evaporated, with a clear view of the enemy, Jackson's artillery and the ships' guns on the river started a relentless shower of grapeshot and cannonball. The British were badly exposed and their small arms were out of range of the Americans, but they continued the advance despite scores of men falling as grapeshot tore into their columns. Captain George Gleig recalled watching his comrades falling as the American guns kept up 'a sweeping fire which cut them down by whole companies'. As the British struggled closer, the Kentucky snipers, along with Choctaw Indians and the rest of the militia, added to the carnage with accurate fire.

It had been less than an hour and with the British attack already faltering, Pakenham realized that Thornton had not yet succeeded on the other bank. In what proved to be a costly mistake, he diverted troops, which had been intended to reinforce the capture of the gun battery on Jackson's right, to the centre. Moving to the left flank, Keane's 93rd Foot (later the Argyll and Sutherland Highlanders) were decimated by the American barrage. Three out of four men were killed; Keane was shot through the neck, but survived. Elsewhere, men were dying in the canal as they try to penetrate the American defences.

Pakenham frantically tried to maintain order as his officers urged forward the remaining troops. Rallying his men, some of whom were now retreating, Pakenham himself led a charge but his horse was shot from under him. His ADC gave him his horse, but on mounting, bullets hit him in the throat and chest. Dying, he was carried to the rear, but not before issuing a final order to General Lambert to bring up the reserves. Lambert pushed forward but made little progress since, with few leaders left, many of the British were now in full retreat. He consequently made the only decision sensibly open to him and took up a defensive position rather than continuing the advance. He was reinforced, no doubt, in this decision by Harry's advice, 'General, the army are in no state to renew the attack. If success now attended so desperate an attempt, we should have no troops to occupy New Orleans; our success even would defeat our object, and, to take an extreme view, which every soldier is bound to do, our whole army might be the sacrifice of so injudicious an assault.' With a thick fog coming on, Harry said, 'We know the enemy are three times our number. They will endeavour immediately to cut off our troops on the right bank, and we may expect an attack in our front. The fog favours us, and Thornton's people ought to be brought back and brought into our line. The army is secure, and no further disaster is to be apprehended.'

Unaware that it was all over on the east side of the river, Thornton was finally in position to attack the American guns under General Morgan. The militia put up a fierce resistance but it was not good enough against an experienced commander like Thornton. His men dealt one blow after another to the American right flank until Morgan's men spiked the guns and retreated. Although Thornton himself was badly wounded, part of his force secured the position while others pursued the Americans more than a mile up the riverbank, until orders from Lambert were received to fall back. The position had become isolated and too difficult to hold under the circumstances. Destroying what guns they could, they recrossed the river and saw, for the first time, the carnage on the battlefield. Sergeant David Brown of the 21st Foot (later the Royal Scots Fusiliers) remembered how 'Many a gallant man and officer wiped the tears from their eyes when they looked back and on their comrades lying in the field.'

The British lost at least 300 dead in the battle; many more of the 1,200 wounded would die later or be maimed for life. The American casualties amounted to only thirteen killed and fifty-two wounded or missing. The Americans took 500 prisoners, but it was the sight of those on the field that made the deepest impression. William Lawrence, an American militiaman, later claimed, 'I could have walked on the dead bodies of the British for one quarter of a mile without stepping on the ground.'

Late that afternoon, Harry was sent to the enemy with a flag of truce and a letter to General Jackson, with a request to be allowed to bury the dead and bring in the wounded lying between their respective positions. The Americans were not accustomed to what Harry called 'the civility of war', unlike the French, and it was some time before they were prepared to allow him to approach. They fired at him, which upset him, especially when a musket ball tore up the ground under his right foot. What annoyed him most was the thought of losing a foot or leg under such circumstances, when the battle was over. An American eyewitness gives this account:

It was near the close of the firing ... there was a white flag raised on the opposite side of the breastwork and the firing ceased. The white flag, before mentioned, was raised about ten or twelve feet from where I stood, close to the breastwork and a little to the right. It was a white handkerchief, or something of the kind, on a sword or stick. It was waved several times, and as soon as it was perceived, we ceased firing. Just then the wind got up a little and blew the smoke off, so that we could see the field. It then appeared that the flag had been raised by a British Officer wearing epaulets. I was told he was a Major. He stepped over the breastwork and came into our lines. Among the Tennesseans who had got mixed with us during the fight, there was a little fellow whose name I do not know; but he was a cadaverous looking chap and went by that of Paleface. As the British Officer came in, Paleface demanded his sword. He hesitated about giving it to him, probably thinking it was derogatory to his dignity to surrender to a private all over begrimed with dust and powder and that some Officer should show him the courtesy to receive it. Just at that moment, Colonel Smiley came up and cried, with a harsh oath, 'Give it up – give it up to him in a minute.' The British Officer quickly handed his weapon to Paleface, holding it in both hands and making a very polite bow. A good many others came in just about the same time.

In the end, Harry received a very courteous reply from General Jackson, who would later become President. After delivering the reply to General Lambert, Harry was again sent out with a large fatigue party with entrenching tools to bury the dead, and some surgeons to examine and bring in the wounded. Harry was met by what he described as a rough fellow, a Colonel Butler, Jackson's Adjutant-General. He had a drawn sword and no scabbard. Butler said, 'Why now, I calculate as your doctors are tired; they have plenty to do to-day.' There was a terrible scene of dead, dying, and wounded around them. '*Do?*' said Harry. 'Why, this is nothing to us Wellington fellows! The next brush we have with you, you shall see how a Brigade of the Peninsula army [arrived the day before] will serve you fellows out with the bayonet. They will lie piled on one another like round shot, if they will only stand.' 'Well, I calculate you must get at 'em first.' 'But,' said Harry, 'what do you carry a drawn sword for?' 'Because I reckon a scabbard of no use so long as one of you Britishers is on our soil. We don't wish to shoot you, but we must, if you molest our property; we have thrown away the scabbard.'

The surgeons by now had arrived. There were some appalling wounds from cannon and grape shot. Harry and his men dug a large pit and threw nearly 200 bodies into it. To the credit of the Americans, not an article of clothing had been taken from the dead, except the shoes. Every body was properly laid out and the large toes tied together with a piece of string, as was the custom.

That night Harry, utterly exhausted and emotionally drained by his day's exertions, lay down wrapped in his cloak at midnight, in General Lambert's room, and was soon fast asleep. Before first light he was up and about, recalling with great sadness the men he loved and admired, particularly General Pakenham, however this was a luxury he could not allow himself for long. Duty called, he mounted his horse and did the rounds of the outposts and sentries. Then he rode to the hospital to check that the Chief Medical Officer had all he needed in the way of orderlies etc. Harry was lavish with his praise for what was being done for the wounded. On returning, he met General Lambert, who said, 'You must have been pretty well done last night, for I did not see you when I lay down.' 'Yes, I had a long day, but we Light Division fellows are used to it,' said Harry, with his customary lack of reticence! Lambert laughed and asked him to be his Military Secretary. It was Harry's turn to laugh and say, 'Me, sir! I write the most illegible and detestable scrawl in the world.' (*Authors' note – agreed!*) 'You can, therefore,' Lambert replied, 'the more readily decipher mine. Poor Pakenham was much attached to you, and strongly recommended you to me.' Up to now Harry had managed to keep his emotions in check, but with all he had recently been through, he burst into a stream of tears. From then on Harry was treated by Lambert as one of the family and, for many years after, the Lambert and Smith families remained in touch.

General Pakenham's remains were put in a cask of spirits and taken home by his Military Secretary, Wylly, who sailed in a few days with dispatches bearing nothing but the gloom of a significant defeat.

'Old Hickory' Jackson wrote the following letter to Lambert just after the battle:

Head Quarters 7h. M. District
Lines below New Orleans
8h Jany 1815. 3 Oclock

Sir,

I have recd. your dispatch of this date. The Army which I have the honor to command have used every exertion to afford relief to the wounded of your Army, even at the constant risque of their lives, your men, never intermitting their fire during such exertions. The wounded now on the field beyond my lines, if you think proper may be taken beyond a line to be designated by my Adjt. General, and be paroled; Otherwise they may be taken to my hospital and treated with every care and attention. The flag sent by Commodore Patterson at my request, has been detained by the Admiral; leaving him uninformed of the fate of his command that was taken in the gunboats – The dead on the field beyond the line, above alluded to, you can inter. Those within that line shall be interred by my troops.

When a return is made of the wounded and prisoners taken on board the Gun boats, and the few men taken on the night of the 23d. it shall be returned by a similar one on my part.

If you should think proper to accede to the above propositions, you will please suggest any arrangement which you may think best for their Accomplishment. I am respectfully &c
A Jackson M G Cg

What none of the contestants knew, at the time, was that this battle, like the Battle of Toulouse before it, was totally unnecessary. The Treaty of Ghent between the United States and Great Britain had been signed on 24 December 1814. However, dispatches giving that news did not arrive until 14 February 1815, and the formal ratification not until 5 March.

Although reinforcements were expected, Lambert decided to re-embark the army and, wisely, abandon the idea of further operations against New Orleans – by now the enemy had greatly added to their strength and carried out considerable works on both banks of the river; they continually shelled the British positions, causing casualties. The

British, uncomfortably, had to deploy a covering force to protect their withdrawal, pretending that they were merely evacuating their wounded. At this stage, Harry was sent forward under a flag of truce to propose an exchange of prisoners. Two companies of the 21st of Foot (later Royal Scots Fusiliers) and many riflemen had managed to climb the American defences but, not being supported by the main body, were easily taken prisoner. Similarly, the British had taken a number of prisoners the night the enemy attacked General Keane.

Harry negotiated the exchange with a Mr Lushington, General Jackson's Military Secretary, an affable and able man. He was, apparently, well known in London, having been Under Secretary of the Legation. Harry enjoyed dealing with this man whom he described as liberal and clear headed. He was not, however, a military expert, and Harry induced him to believe that Lambert's force had no intention of abandoning the conflict. During the afternoon, when the prisoner exchanges were completed, Harry said, 'We shall soon meet in New Orleans, and after that in London.' Lushington was evidently impressed with the idea that the British intended to attack again and Harry led him to believe that a night attack would be most likely. Nevertheless, they parted the best of friends and kept up correspondence down the years.

On 18 January, as soon as it was dark, the British began to move off; by midnight all patrols were in and the withdrawal was successfully under way. The enemy heard them and opened fire in the belief that a night attack was about to take place. Luckily the fire was ineffective and, although uncomfortably up to their necks in mud and water, Lambert's men managed to get away unscathed over the next three days.

Once they had rested and recovered, Lambert resolved to take the town of Mobile.

An irritant, in the form of the small Fort Bowyer, lay at the mouth of the Mobile Bay, the taking of which would not present much of a military problem but would be an unnecessary distraction and inevitable loss of life. Nevertheless, it could not be bypassed. Harry was therefore sent by Lambert to negotiate the surrender. There then followed a hilarious exchange between Harry and the commander of the Fort, a Major Lawrence, who clearly had never met anyone quite like Harry before.

One cannot improve on Harry's version:

> The Major was as civil as a vulgar fellow can be. I gave him my
> version of his position and cheered him on the ability he had
> displayed. He (Major Lawrence) said, 'Well, now, I calculate you
> are not far out in your reckoning. What do you advise me to do?
> You, I suppose, are one of Wellington's men, and understand the
> rules in these cases.' 'This,' I said, 'belongs to the rule that the
> weakest goes to the wall, and if you do not surrender at discretion
> in one hour, we, being the stronger, will blow up the fort and burn
> your wooden walls about your ears.'

The fort surrendered.

Two days later the dispatches arrived with the news of the Treaty of
Ghent and it was decided, pending Ratification, to disembark the troops
on a large island at the entrance of Mobile Bay, called Isle Dauphine. At
first they had great difficulty in obtaining fresh provisions, but as the sea
was full of fish, nets were put out and large catches achieved. Biscuit ran
short and, while flour was plentiful, it was giving men dysentery. Harry
then hit on the idea of making an oven from a mortar compound of
burnt oyster shells and sand, in which to bake bread. This proved such
a success that he was able to hold a breakfast party for the Admiral and
the generals at which freshly baked bread was produced. Harry's
innovation, of course, was copied by the regiments and round the Fleet
to everyone's satisfaction.

Harry's morale was further raised as, with the dispatches, came a
letter from Juana, dying for his return and telling him of the love his
family had for her. Harry, for his part, now that peace was assured, could
not want anything more.

With the Ratification confirmed, the force now happily sailed for home
via Havana to re-provision. They spent a week there and Harry's expert
Spanish was, again, put to much use, particularly in conversation with
the ladies. General Lambert, Harry and his friends also met the
celebrated Mr Woodville, a cigar maker. He asked them to breakfast at
his house, 4 or 5 miles out of the town. He was about six feet two, a big
powerful man, with lots of snow-white hair, the picture of health and

with a voice of thunder. He was rough, but hospitable, and after breakfast showed them his factory and the processes each cigar went through. 'Now,' he said, 'Sir John, I have another sight to show you, which few men can boast of.' Putting his fingers in his mouth, he blew a loud whistle, whereupon from every direction ran lots of happy, healthy-looking children of various different colours. None of them appeared to be older than twelve or thirteen. 'Ah, report says, and I believe it, they are every one of them my children. Count them,' he said to Harry. He did; there were forty-one. Harry and his friends laughed merrily. Sir John Lambert, a highly moral and amiable soul, mildly put it, 'A very large family indeed, Mr Woodville.' That convulsed them again and the old patriarch joined in the laughter with, 'Ah, the seed of Abraham would people the earth indeed, if every one of his descendants could show my family.'

After a pretty rough transatlantic crossing, Harry's ship was nearing the mouth of the Bristol Channel when they encountered a merchantman sailing in the opposite direction, and shouted, 'What news?' as they passed. 'No, none.' Then, as the ship was pulling away, a voice shouted, 'Bonaparte's back on the throne of France.' Harry's reaction was to shout for joy and throw his hat in the air. 'I will be a Lieutenant Colonel before the year is out!' Lambert's reaction was less enthusiastic and rather more measured. He found it difficult to believe but realized the merchantman's captain was hardly likely to make up such a story. Anyway, when they arrived at Spithead, the bustle and activity made it quite clear that much was afoot. Lambert and Harry left for London but only got as far as Guildford, when Harry's exasperation and impatience got the better of him and he asked Lambert if he could press on by himself. Lambert was reluctant but allowed him to go, with the proviso that Harry wrote to him, with his address, saying, darkly, that he would no doubt have need of him again very soon. So Harry and his orderly, West, sped on for London where the former just had time to get a few presents for his wife, saying to himself that, as he also had some Spanish books from Havana, he was not going to arrive home as empty handed as he had done after Corunna. 'Naked and penniless' was how he put it.

Galloping on with a coach-and-four, they reached the Falcon Inn, which still exists today in Whittlesey. Harry was in such a state of nervous excitement that he did not want to go straight to his father's house, so instead sent for him to come to the inn, which he shortly did. They had passed the church and, it being a Sunday, Harry realized that Juana and his sisters would be attending the service, and that they customarily took a stroll after church. Word was then sent that Harry's father wanted to see them. Unfortunately, the messenger who found them blurted out that there was a man with their father who he did not know, who had arrived post haste from London. Unsurprisingly, Juana immediately assumed this to be an officer bringing bad news of Harry's death and fell into a swoon. However, all was unravelled and Juana, revived by his sisters, joyously fell into Harry's arms – never again to be separated.

# Chapter 5

# Waterloo
# March 1815 to January 1829

When Harry returned to Whittlesey that March, he found Juana surrounded by an affectionate and loving family, but excited at the prospect of serving once again under the Duke – after all, he had given her away at her wedding in Badajoz. Harry wrote: 'All was now excitement, joy, hope and animation, and preparation of riding-habits, tents, canteens etc, my sisters thinking of all sorts of things for my wife's comfort, which we could as well have carried as our parish church.' Harry had to purchase horses both for himself and for Juana, and to organize their whole trip. Sir John Lambert wrote to confirm that Harry would be his Brigade Major, and suggested that as he was in Cambridgeshire he should cross to Brussels via Harwich and Ostend. The night before they left, the whole family went for a ride on their horses. Harry was riding an old favourite and – always liable to show off – rode at a high fence, but the horse failed, rolled on top of him and pinned down his leg. He had visions of the end of his military career but, amazingly, he emerged unharmed except for severe bruising, and so they set off to take part in what would be the final showdown with Napoleon – the Battle of Waterloo.

Waterloo was, without question, the epic battle of the nineteenth century, and, although it lasted only a day and was fought over ground not much bigger than Hyde Park, it resulted in the final destruction of the Napoleonic Empire. To Harry's chagrin, he did not fight with his beloved 95th (after the battle to be renamed the Rifle Brigade), but found himself on the staff in Lambert's Brigade Headquarters. Nevertheless, he played a not insignificant role, as we shall see.

On 1 March 1815, Napoleon had escaped from Elba and landed in France. Nineteen days later he was in Paris and resumed his title as Emperor; his army rallied to him. The soldiers who had been captured during the years of earlier fighting had been released and they enabled Napoleon to reform his Grande Armée. The European allies reassembled their armies and prepared to resume the war to overthrow the Emperor yet again. Napoleon resolved to attack the British, Prussian, Belgian and Dutch armies before the other powers could come to their assistance, and marched into Belgium.

Harry and Juana, together with his brother, Charles, arrived in Ghent, having spent some frustrating days waiting for good weather in Harwich. Harry was raring to go but also reported that Juana was 'delighted to be once more in campaigning trim'. Having met up with General Lambert, Harry was pleased to see that the Brigade consisted of what he called the New Orleans regiments, including three of the best battalions, in his view, of the old Peninsula regiments. Shortly, the Brigade was ordered to march towards Brussels and arrived at Asche on the afternoon of 16 June, from where gunfire from Quatre Bras could be clearly heard. This action was due to an early move by Napoleon to have Marshal Ney sever the forward link between Wellington and Blücher. The result was some heavy fighting, but any French success was thwarted by Wellington's tactical withdrawal, bar a rearguard, towards his favoured position along the line of the Mont St Jean ridge to the south of Waterloo. He was now well set as long as the Prussians turned up. Meanwhile, the fog of war had descended on Harry's Brigade. Soldiers rushed to alarm positions, bugles sounded and troopers galloped hither and thither in a high state of excitement. Rumours of French penetration of their positions were rife, but the experienced troops kept cool heads, including Harry and his Brigade Commander who calmly sat down to dinner with Juana and the ADC.

At nightfall it poured with rain and this was to have a significant effect on the coming battle. Roads and villages became a muddy, seething mass of guns and their limbers, struggling horses, bogged-down wagons and swearing soldiery trying to make their way forward. On the morning of 18 June, having consolidated the Brigade position, Lambert sent Harry to locate the Duke and obtain orders. About 11.00am, he found him with his staff, near the Hougoumont farm, later to be the scene of some of the heaviest fighting by the Brigade of Guards in the battle. Recognizing Harry, the Duke asked him news of his Brigade. Harry replied in his characteristically robust and confident way, emphasizing the qualities of his regiments. At that point, one of Wellington's staff officers suggested that the French were unlikely to attack that day. 'Nonsense,' the Duke replied, 'the columns are already forming and we shall be attacked within the hour.' How right he was. Turning to Harry, he asked if he had noted the junction of the main roads between Genappe and Nivelles, on his way up. Harry indeed had and so the Duke told him to bring the Brigade forward to that crossroads. Thereafter, Lambert was to be prepared to assume a position on the left, between the Nassau Brigade and Picton's Division, taking under command a newly raised brigade of Hanoverians. Despite all the pressures on him, Wellington took great care, coolly and deliberately, to ensure that Harry understood exactly what was required and, furthermore, Harry himself was to reconnoitre the shortest and most suitable route for Lambert's Brigade to move, when ordered, to this new position.

No sooner had Harry returned to the Brigade Headquarters than the battle started. Lying behind the ridge, it was difficult to see what was going on and at one stage a whole lot of panicking Dutch soldiers ran through the ranks of Lambert's Brigade, making it look as though retreat was a possibility. Some dragoons, charging through their lines with prisoners and captured French Eagles, caused added confusion. However, the Brigade was soon ordered to take up the position that the Duke had given Harry earlier that morning. Historians, with the benefit of hindsight and careful analysis, are tempted to write tidy accounts of battles and manoeuvres, but the reality, for ordinary soldiers, is one of fear, anxiety, muddle, disorientation and lack of communication. Half the time they had no idea of what was happening. Despite his position in the Brigade Headquarters, Harry was no exception. The smoke lay so thick over the battlefield, it was impossible to see where any formed body of troops was or, for that matter, the difference between friend or foe. Towards the end of the day, although firing had ceased, Harry admitted he had no idea who had won. It was not until he identified a French column withdrawing in disarray before some Redcoats, and heard a very British cry of triumph, that he realized the day was theirs. Through the smoke, Harry was spotted by the Duke of Wellington. 'Where are your people? Tell them to form companies and move on immediately.' Harry replied, 'In which direction, my lord?' He had completely lost his bearings in the fog. Wellington pointed, 'Why, right ahead.' Harry did so, but the battle was over. (Possibly one of the last cannon balls to be fired by the French took off Lord Uxbridge's leg, leading to the probably apocryphal remark of Wellington's, 'Have you, by God?' in response to Uxbridge's 'By God, I've lost my leg!' It is sometimes quoted to demonstrate Wellington's hard-heartedness, but this is to misunderstand soldiers' reactions in the heat of battle when there is little room for emotion and the niceties of good manners or sympathy.)

Then came the dreadful reckoning. Harry, having had two horses shot under him but not killed, remained unscathed, as were his two brothers, Charles and Tom, fighting respectively in the 1st and 2nd Battalions of the 95th, although Charles received a minor flesh wound in the neck. However, the carnage overall was appalling: dead were piled upon dead, the screams of the wounded and dying rent the air, and scavengers were already at work, stripping bodies of anything of value. One of the regiments in Harry's Brigade, the 27th (later the Royal Inniskilling Fusiliers) lost all their officers bar two, and they were wounded. When the Battalion was down to barely 120 men, legend has it that the initiative was seized by an officer in the 95th which was close by, a Lieutenant Archie Stewart, who rallied the remnants and led them in a charge against the French. The officer's descendants have his medals among which, together with the Waterloo medal and the order of the Knight of Hanover, there is, curiously, a French Legion d'Honneur. Family history fails to record how he came by the latter.

Harry gave his own description of Waterloo:

> I had been over many a field of battle, but with the exception of one spot at New Orleans, and the breach of Badajoz, I had never

seen anything to be compared with what I saw. At Waterloo the whole field from right to left was a mass of dead bodies. In one spot, to the right of La Haye Sainte, the French Cuirassiers were literally piled on each other; many soldiers not wounded lying under their horses; others, fearfully wounded, occasionally with their horses struggling upon their wounded bodies. The sight was sickening, and I had no means or power to assist them. Imperative duty compelled me to the field of my comrades, where I had plenty to do to assist many who had been left out all night; some had been believed to be dead, but the spark of life had returned. All over the field you saw officers, and as many soldiers as were permitted to leave the ranks, leaning and weeping over some dead or dying brother or comrade.

A number of Harry's friends were killed or wounded. He found Captain McCulloch, an old colleague from Peninsula days, in great agony from wounds in the arm and back, wounds that were over and above the seven sabre cuts he had sustained at the Coa, where Harry had been shot in the ankle. Amazingly, McCulloch recovered, but sadly died of dysentery some time later. For Harry, the post-trauma drop in adrenaline level and the appalling losses (Allies 22,000, French 41,000) put him into a dark mood of dejection when, as many soldiers do in similar circumstances, he had his doubts and asked himself whether he was doing the right thing. However, the body and mind can recover swiftly and, after a good night's sleep, Harry regained his usual cheerful and ebullient nature.

Predictably, Harry had his own forthright views on why the battle was won. He takes the Prussians to task for arriving late, thereby seriously jeopardizing the Allies' left flank. This is not quite how Wellington saw it though, writing: 'I should not do justice to my own feelings, or to Marshal Blücher and the Prussian army, if I did not attribute the successful result of this arduous day to the cordial and timely assistance I received from them. The operation of General Bulow upon the enemy's flank was a most decisive one.' Harry roundly criticizes Napoleon for: 'fighting the battle badly'; partial and isolated attacks; sacrificing his cavalry too early; and failing to turn the Allies' flank. However, he goes on to praise the French artillery and cavalry, but denigrates the infantry. He was right that Waterloo lacked the brilliant manoeuvring of Salamanca and Vitoria, but at Waterloo there was no time for the famous Napoleonic sweep, due to boggy and difficult terrain – he had to act swiftly but Wellington was stolidly ready for him. Wellington's army was composed of relatively raw troops and unreliable allies, not the seasoned veterans of the Peninsula, apart from a few battalions, such as the 95th, of course; but they stood their ground and did what they had to do. At the end of the day, Wellington's infantry lines held together better than Napoleon's, his firepower was better organized and his generals were better than Napoleon's marshals. Let Wellington have the last word: 'Never did I see such a pounding match. Both were what boxers call gluttons. Napoleon did not manoeuvre at all. He just moved forward in the old style, in columns, and was driven off in the old style.' From then on, officers appearing in the Army List, who had fought at Waterloo, were to have a Gothic 'w' in front of their names.

Harry's thoughts now naturally turned to Juana. He had left her in Brussels early on 18 June and knew she would be worried about him. How had she been and what fears would she have suffered? He was desperate to reach her and assure her of his safety. On 17 June, when the preliminary battles had already been fought, Harry and Juana had dinner with Sir John Lambert, Harry's Brigade Commander. Harry – well informed as ever – realized that the final showdown between Wellington and Napoleon was about to take place, and ordered Juana and West to go back to Brussels to await the outcome of the battle. All the fears and agony which she suffered when her Enrique went into a battle were instantly revived. She pleaded not to be sent back, but the steely note in his voice when he said 'That is an order' made her realize that she had to obey, and after a final embrace they parted.

Juana and West left at once and returned to Brussels, where in the centre of the city there was complete chaos, because orders had been given for all civilians and all the army baggage to be moved off towards Antwerp. They rode on along the crowded road and in the early evening reached a village where they hoped to stay the night. Suddenly the alarm was raised and the rumour spread that the French were advancing upon them. In a scene of high tension, West brought her horse for Juana, but the horse was frantic. She tried to calm it, but when West handed her

1. The Register of Baptisms and Burials at Whittlesey, showing Harry's entry on 14 August 1787, proving that he was born in 1787, not 1788. (*WM*)

2. The rear view of Harry's house in Whittlesey. (*WM*)

3. The plaque on the wall of Aliwal House in Whittlesey, showing the incorrect year of birth.

4. The house today, from the street.

5. Portrait of Harry, probably about 1815. (*Biog.*)

6. Portrait of Juana in a pink dress in 1815. By Jean-Baptiste Isaby (1767–1855). (*Biog.*)

7. Harry's Waterloo medal now at the Rifles' Museum at Winchester. The original was looted by Sikhs from the baggage train at Budowal. Harry's was replaced in 1847. There is also one in the main collection of his medals. Both have his name on the rim but, unlike nowadays, are not engraved 'Replacement'. So which is genuine? (*RM*)

8. Harry's Peninsula medal, with twelve clasps. The medal was not issued until 1847. Unlike today, if a participant in a battle died before the medal was issued, his descendants would not receive it. (*CR*)

Harry from the portrait in the Rifles' Museum, Winchester. (*RM*)

10. Busts of Harry and Juana. They were sculpted at the same time and were never separated. (CR

11. Dispatch after the Battle of Aliwal in Harry's handwriting. (*RM*)

2. List of awards after Aliwal. As there were no gallantry decorations in those days, officers were promoted to 'brevet' rank or, if senior enough, made Companions of the Order of the Bath (CB) or ADC to the Queen. (*WM*)

13. Juana painted by Mrs Henry Moseley in September 1847. (*CR*)

14. Juana's medals. The Maharajpore medal is below, and the medal Harry had made into a brooch is above. (*CR*)

15. Harry's beloved charger, Aliwal. Painted in 1847. (*CR*)

16. Harry in pen and wash, wearing sash and order of GCB. (*CR*)

17. Harry in later life, wearing his Order and sash. (*CR*)

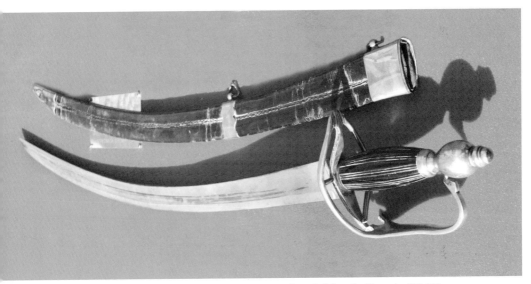

8. Sword and scabbard hanging below Harry's memorial in St Mary's Church, Whittlesey.

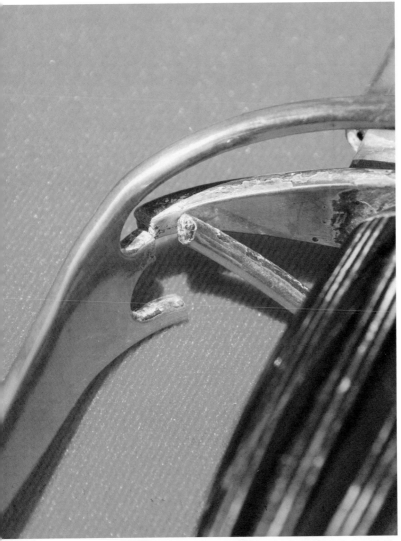

19. Sword showing the damage to the basket/hilt.

20. Harry's memorial in the south-east chapel of St Mary's.

21. St Mary's Church, Whittlesey, today.

2. Harry in the twilight of his years. Note the now mandatory moustache, and sideboards. Juana
rather approved. (*CR*)

23. Tower of the San Domingo Convent in Buenos Aires today, still showing marks of British cannon balls. (*Eduardo Gerding*)

24. The original 'Hero of Aliwal' pub in Whittlesey, long since gone. (*WM*)

. Harry's medals and orders.

ft: GCB Order and sash.

ght: Portugese Order and sash of Grand Cross of St Bento d'Aviz.

ft to right at the top: Waterloo, KCB and CB, Maharajpore.

ntre: Sutlej (Moodkee on medal, Sobraon, Aliwal, Ferozeshah clasps), Peninsula (Clasps of ulouse, Orthes, Nive, Nivelle, Pyrenees, Vitoria, Salamanca, Badajoz, Ciudad Rodrigo, Fuentes Onoro Busaco, Corunna), South Africa 1853.

ntre below: Miniatures. (*CR*)

. Plate on side of Harry's tomb.

IN THE HOUSE OF LORDS, 3º APRIL 1846, THE DUKE OF WELLINGTON SAID —

"I WILL SAY MY LORDS, WITH REGARD TO THE MOVEMENTS OF SIR HARRY SMITH, THAT I HAVE READ THE ACCOUNTS OF MANY BATTLES, BUT NEVER READ AN ACCOUNT OF ANY AFFAIR IN WHICH ANY OFFICER HAS EVER SHEWN HIMSELF MORE CAPABLE THAN THIS OFFICER DID OF COMMANDING TROOPS IN THE FIELD, OR IN WHICH EVERY DESCRIPTION OF TROOPS HAS BEEN BROUGHT TO BEAR WITH ITS ARM IN THE POSITION IN WHICH IT WAS MOST CAPABLE OF RENDERING SERVICE OR IN WHICH EVERY THING WAS CARRIED ON MORE PERFECTLY; THE NICEST MANŒUVRES BEING PERFORMED UNDER THE ENEMY'S FIRE WITH THE UTMOST PRECISION. I MUST SAY OF THIS OFFICER THAT I NEVER SAW ANY CASE OF ABILITY MANIFESTED MORE CLEARLY THAN IN THIS CASE: IT HAS BEEN SHEWN THAT SIR HARRY SMITH IS AN OFFICER CAPABLE OF RENDERING THE MOST IMPORTANT SERVICES, AND ULTIMATELY OF BEING AN HONOR TO HIS COUNTRY"

27 Harry and Iuana's tomb in the Whittlesey cemetery

faithful little pug, Vitty, up to her the rein slipped from her grasp and the horse galloped off, crashing through crowds of horses, wagons and frightened people. This desperate ride went on for about 8 miles until the horse, suddenly facing an overturned wagon, finally came to an abrupt halt, nearly pitching Juana and Vitty off on to the ground. This at least allowed her to control the horse and stop the gallop. When she set off again, a group of horsemen rode up; she assumed that they were French and would take her prisoner, but fortunately they were British troops, including an Hussar officer who, without stopping, said that the French were close behind and that they should hurry on towards Antwerp. Another man told her to throw away the dog, which infuriated her.

Juana reached Antwerp with the Hussar, and he did try to find her a billet, but the town was choked with civilians – mostly British – who had fled from Brussels, and she had to go to the Hotel de Ville to seek accommodation. She waited, feeling acutely embarrassed, later describing her appearance: 'I was wet from head to foot with the black mud of the high-road. On my face the mud had dried, and a flood of tears chasing each other through it down my cheeks must have given me an odd appearance indeed.' Then another officer approached and, seeing her plight, offered to take her to the family home of Colonel Craufurd, Commandant of the garrison. To her great relief, Mrs Craufurd, who had two daughters, gave her a warm welcome, a bath, dry clothes and a meal.

The following morning, 19 June, the officer who had brought Juana to the Craufurds returned with West, their horses and their baggage. All through the day came news of a great battle with very heavy casualties, and Juana became increasingly alarmed and apprehensive. In spite of the entreaties of her kind hostess, she determined to leave at 3.00am next day to ride to the battlefield and find news of Harry. Before they left, she and West had a mild dispute with the innkeeper over where their goods had been left, and managed to recover a valuable dressing case and other items. Then, travelling light, they galloped off and reached Brussels by 7.00am. There they found soldiers of the Rifles who, to Juana's horror, told her that Brigade Major Smith had been killed. Juana later wrote:

> In a state approaching desperation I urged the horse to the utmost speed to the field of battle to seek my husband's corpse ... the road was nearly choked which was to lead me to the completion,

as I hoped, of my life; to die on the body of the only thing I had on earth to love, and which I loved with a faithfulness which few can or ever did feel. In my agony of woe, I approached the awful field of Sunday's carnage, in a mad search for Enrique.

When she reached the battlefield, she soon saw the carnage, with wagons, guns, uniforms and equipment all destroyed, and everywhere the smell of death. Then, adding to her horror, she saw deep pits full of corpses and other hastily dug graves, and dreaded the thought that Harry was already buried and she would never see him again. In the extremity of her grief, she recalled her convent upbringing and she prayed to God through Jesus Christ. Soon afterwards – not exactly claiming a miracle – she came face to face with one of their closest friends from the Peninsula, Charlie Gore. She rushed to him, begging to be told where she could find Harry's body.

Charlie replied that Harry was a few miles away, unwounded and as fit as he had ever been. Juana, having been told of his certain death, begged Charlie not to deceive her. Sensing her frantic and overwrought state, he quickly confirmed that the Brigade Major of another brigade – also called Smith – had indeed been killed, but Harry and both his brothers had all come through safely. He swore on his honour that Harry was well and even then was riding his favourite horse Lochinvar. Charlie was about to ride off to Mons to find Harry and so Juana accompanied him. Through a day of anguish and emotional turmoil, she had been in the saddle since 3 o'clock that morning, and when they reached Mons she had ridden for 60 miles. They found shelter and she slept briefly. Then at daybreak on 21 June, they hurried on to Bavay where she saw Sir John Lambert, who told her where she would find Harry. She wrote:

Until I saw him, I could not persuade myself that he was well, such a hold had my previous horror taken of my every thought and feeling. Soon, O gracious God, I sank into his embrace, exhausted, fatigued, happy, and grateful – oh how grateful – to God who had protected him and sustained my reason through such scenes of carnage, horror, dread, and belief in my bereavement.

As Europe now settled into a long peace of nearly forty years, Harry and

Juana were to have one of the happiest periods of their lives – a round of parties, hunting, good food and wine, fine clothes and mingling with the aristocracy, in particular, Harry's hero, the Duke of Wellington. Harry now became a senior staff officer in General Lowry Cole's 6th Division, being responsible for the administration of some 17,000 men. Although by nature more of a front-line soldier, he clearly enjoyed the job and could get his teeth into real day-to-day problems of an Army of Occupation. Juana and he settled comfortably into the country residence in Neuilly of a Parisian lady with whom they made firm friends. To Harry's great satisfaction he was promoted to Lieutenant Colonel and made a Companion of the Order of the Bath – a fitting reward for his considerable wartime experience and, by any standards, exemplary service.

During the autumn, the Division had to move into more permanent accommodation in St Germain, which Harry described in his autobiography as the magnificent and ancient resort of former kings. Stag hunting, in the French style, was all the rage and although one can sense Harry's disdain for what he considered to be a dandified chase, he nevertheless took it up with enthusiasm. Accompanied, of course, by Juana, now an accomplished and stylish horsewoman, Harry fell in with the irascible Duc de Berri, thundering up and down the forest rides on huge horses. Typically, Harry did not approve of the French hunting customs and conventions, nor did he really like de Berri whom he clearly thought a lightweight. So, with his friend, Will Havelock, he collected sufficient foxhounds from various sources to form a very creditable pack.

Under the terms of the resumed Congress of Vienna, four British Divisions were to remain stationed in northern France for the next three years, the bulk of the army being garrisoned in the Valenciennes area, with Wellington's headquarters in Cambrai. With the reduction in strength of the 6th Division, Harry was posted back to his Regiment in his permanent rank of Major. His fellow officers wondered how he would take this reduction in authority and status but, as ever, he had the steadfast support of his old friend, Charlie Beckwith, who had no doubts that Harry would happily revert to being an outstanding company commander. On the move again, the Smiths found themselves quarters in a large, cold chateau accompanied, nevertheless, by his pack of hounds. Harry was then sent for by his Commanding Officer who told him that the Regiment had to provide a Captain for the Depot at Shornecliffe and, unfortunately, Harry was their nomination. This filled him with gloom – particularly at the thought of the lower income in the United Kingdom, when he had become accustomed to the relatively high life of continental living. He did not dare tell Juana.

However, all was well as no sooner had they reached Bourlon, near Cambrai, when Harry was summoned by General Lambert who told him that plans had changed and he had been ordered to find a major who, with an Engineer officer, was to take over the town of Cambrai from the French, together with all its stores, weapons and materiel. Harry was to be that major. He was overjoyed and, forgetting Shornecliffe with alacrity, started for Cambrai early the following morning. He was to be the Town Major of Cambrai and Charlie Beckwith that of Valenciennes, both with the pay of Assistant Quartermaster-General. His dreams had come true.

Almost as soon as he had settled into his new job, he was summoned by the Duke of Wellington and told to bring with him a map of the surrounding area of Cambrai. Accordingly, with some nervousness, he approached the Headquarters, wondering why the Duke had called him. But it was all about hunting. Seizing the map, the Duke asked where the foxes were. Harry showed him and the Duke then drew a boundary line across the map, saying to Harry, 'Your hounds hunt that side, mine this.' Foxhounds were not the only interest they shared for Harry also obtained greyhounds for coursing hares (it will be remembered that in the Peninsula he often spent time coursing, with particular benefit to the stewpot). Naturally, Juana joined in and was universally admired for her horsemanship and courage. Much enjoyable sport was had and friendly rivalry between Harry's 'Spanish' hounds and those brought out from England.

The relationship between Harry and Wellington was interestingly close. On the one hand, Harry, a mere major in an infantry regiment, albeit with a considerable wartime reputation, and on the other, the Duke, the Commander-in-Chief at the very pinnacle of his military career, before taking up a political one. Yet Wellington clearly enjoyed Harry's company, his outspoken views, enthusiasm and joie de vivre. He also, doubtless, admired Juana's loyalty and spirit, perhaps her loveliness too, not being averse to a pretty face. Despite his self-confidence, which at times verged on arrogance, Harry was nevertheless careful not to presume too much on the Duke's favour. Riding home together one day, the conversation turned to hunting on Sundays, which Harry deplored. The Duke went on to mull over battles that they had both fought, often occurring on a Sunday. Harry reminded him of Trafalgar and New Orleans, both happening on a Sunday, let alone Agincourt which had been fought 400 years before, to the day. He suddenly remembered that the Duke's brother-in-law, General Edward Pakenham, had been killed at New Orleans and became nervous of hurting the Duke's feelings by mentioning him, although as he had admired Pakenham enormously, he wanted to tell the Duke so. However the Duke happily discussed the battle, demonstrating a complete grasp of detail and the way in which it had been fought. Years later, when Harry received an honorary degree at Cambridge University, the Vice-Chancellor commented that the Duke looked on Harry almost as a son.

In Harry's view the Duke could do no wrong, whether he was, in the best of spirits, coursing with his old Army cronies, or representing his country, dining with the crowned heads of Europe. At one ball, attended by the Russian Prince and Princess Narinska, together with a number of other Russian and Cossack officers, Wellington wished the mazurka to be danced in the honour of the Princess, who was the only Russian lady present. As the English ladies were not up to it, the Duke turned to Juana and invited her to dance this 'Russian fandango' as he put it. Juana, not one to refuse a challenge, cheerfully accepted and danced quite beautifully with a Russian officer, partnering the Princess, to the admiration of the Duke, and Harry's great pride.

One night, riding into Valenciennes, on a road thronged by troops marching back to barracks, it was bitterly cold and Harry was clapping his arms onto his shoulders to keep warm. Suddenly Juana said, 'You have lost your Star of the Bath.' He had felt something catch in the lace of his sleeve, so he turned back. A column of Russian Cuirassiers was marching along the road he had just ridden over. Since it was dark and the road was filthy, he thought that he could not possibly find it and was in the act of turning back to Juana, when a flat-footed Dragoon horse, having stood on it, kicked it up under his own horse's nose, out of the dirt on the street. He was absolutely astonished and delighted. Although the Star was dented by the horse's foot, he wore it like that, unrepaired, for the next twenty-nine years.

The British occupation of France was one of benign autocracy; the inhabitants were well treated, misdemeanours by British troops were punished and materiel properly paid for. Harry and Juana had a wonderful time. He was the Master of a superb pack of hounds, a dashing steeplechaser and a racing steward. She was beautiful, admired by the Duke, who called her his Spanish heroine, and could dance and sing with the best. Once, Wellington proudly presented her to the Emperor of Russia as 'ma petite guerrière espagnole'. Speaking fluent French, she rode with the Emperor and amused him with anecdotes of the Peninsula War. However, all this did not come cheap and Harry ruefully admitted that, despite his prize money from Washington, the Peninsular and Waterloo, together with an inheritance from his grandmother, he was running into debt.

By 1818, the Occupation was drawing to a close and Harry, with a Home posting in sight, was forced to concentrate on his perilous financial position. There was nothing for it but to raffle one of his best horses, Lochinvar. The horse had been bought for him by his father just before Waterloo and was a fine animal of some 16 hands. Juana insisted, despite Harry's protestations, on buying a ticket. Needless to say, her ticket won, Harry was richer by 245 Napoleons and kept his horse. History does not reveal what the other punters thought of this!

Harry and Juana thus bid a sad farewell to the Frenchman on whom they had been billeted for nearly three years. The local Mayor made an impassioned speech that, while expressing relief at now being free from occupation, nevertheless praised the British for their generosity and impartiality. What did home and the United Kingdom now hold in store for them?

In October 1818, Harry and Juana returned to an England which was reeling from the financial strain of the Napoleonic wars; unemployment and poverty were endemic, particularly among discharged soldiers and officers reduced to half-pay. Coupled with an outdated electoral system of Rotten and Pocket Boroughs, this led, inevitably, to widespread social dissatisfaction and disruption.

Harry was posted to the 1st Battalion of his Regiment at Shornecliffe, initially to command a company of recruits. After a brief spell at Gosport with the Battalion, they returned to Shornecliffe, which had been the Depot throughout the war. He was then put in command of Headquarter Company. Juana was able to stay with the family of their old friend, General Lambert. Despite keeping his hunter, Lochinvar, which Juana had 'won' in the raffle, an additional mare and Juana's favourite horse, they managed to live on his pay of 12s 6d a day. Old campaign habits died hard though, and Harry and his men often looked over the Kent countryside, theoretically assessing its defensive possibilities against the now non-existent French invasion. They concluded that the French would never have made it to London if they had had anything to do with it. Oddly, Harry found that sentries were still being posted until he raised the matter further up the line and the procedure was stopped. There were sad partings from old soldiers now being discharged to an uncertain future. Many had been through battles, not only with Harry, but also with Juana, whom they loved and admired. An emotional Waterloo Dinner was held, Harry's first in England, to commemorate the victory and remember the Fallen.

Disturbances now started to occur in the industrial cities of Manchester, Birmingham and Glasgow. Harry and the 1st Battalion were sent north by ship and landed at Leith Docks, Edinburgh, on 27 September 1819, from where they were deployed to Glasgow 'In Aid of the Civil Power'. Juana lived with Harry in barracks in pretty indifferent conditions until lodgings were found for her with the 94-year-old Mrs Beckwith, mother of a number of famous soldier sons, including Harry's friend, Charlie. The old lady was fascinated to learn Juana was Spanish and insisted on her showing her legs and ankles as she had heard that Spanish ladies were well known for their 'neatness'.

Harry and his men had a tiresome and thankless task in Glasgow of the sort well known to modern British soldiers, until recently, in Northern Ireland. Often insulted and jostled by the mob, the riflemen, nevertheless, retained their temper and composure, gaining the grudging respect of the local population, some of whom were old soldiers themselves, eking out a sub-standard existence. Typically, Harry was deployed on one occasion to make several arrests, whereupon a crowd gathered and became violent. Harry put the prisoners in the middle of his Company and covered their withdrawal to barracks with a troop of Hussars. Unlike the 'massacre of Peterloo' in Manchester in August 1819, where the terrified Magistrates read the Riot Act and ordered troops to disperse the crowds with force, resulting in considerable violence and a number of deaths, the Glaswegian Magistrates were more robust. Harry, therefore, properly ordered his Hussars merely to lay about the mob with the flat of their swords. He did not, however, escape censure from the pompous and self-important Lord Advocate for allowing his troops to be 'insulted with impunity'. But Harry was not having any of this. He explained, quite clearly, that he was acting under the direction of the Magistrates and had no intention of unnecessarily shedding the blood of innocent people when his mission (of arresting and conveying the prisoners into custody) could be accomplished without acting like those in Manchester. If the Lord Advocate wished – and one can almost hear Harry's sardonic tone – he only had to give the order, in writing of course, and Harry would march the prisoners, under military escort, back through Glasgow. This would provoke a predictable riot and possible rescue attempt, at which point Harry would open fire on the citizens of Glasgow. Is that what he wanted? With a 'Good morning, my Lord', Harry turned on his heel and left, no doubt with a contemptuous curl of the lip.

This hardly slowed Harry's career because he was soon appointed Brigade Major of the military district and he thus, once more, returned to the Staff, not to leave it again until 1825. He reported directly to the General Officer Commanding in Edinburgh, Sir Thomas Bradford, to the consternation of several officers more senior to him. Life took on a more congenial pattern as he spent much time travelling throughout Scotland inspecting Yeomanry and Militia, and accepting much hospitality from the local gentry. His exotic Spanish wife was a great asset and a source of considerable admiration from the Scottish aristocracy. Harry was a great supporter of what we would now call the Territorial Army and saw nothing but good coming from the mixture of social classes within the ranks. Lairds and labourers joined together with enormous dash and enthusiasm.

When King George IV visited Edinburgh in August 1822, Harry was put in charge of the military arrangements. This was a significant honour and Harry and Juana much enjoyed the social affairs that went with such great occasions. Harry confessed to being agreeably surprised by the charm and efficiency of the courtiers and royal staff. He clearly had a typically jaundiced, front-line soldier's view of the flunkey and obsequious world of the Court and those who worked within it. He also ruefully admitted that his new uniforms and court dresses for Juana cost him a year's salary; nevertheless, 'His Majesty particularly admired my wife's riding.'

Harry briefly went back to Paris in 1824 to 'arrange a little matter of delicacy with a gentleman who had ill-treated a lady', the latter being a friend of a friend. History does not relate what this delicate matter was but it was satisfactorily concluded and Harry enjoyed seeing all the changes that had taken place since he had been there in 1815. He happily returned to Britain, his own country, which he loved and to the soldiers he admired so much. Juana had no family left in Spain but one wonders whether Harry ever allowed her to think of returning for a visit. By 1825 the troubles had largely evaporated and were to be even further calmed, although not totally, by the later Reform Bill of 1832. Harry, therefore, was no longer required as Brigade Major and returned to his Regiment, now in Ireland. The contrast between the grime of Glasgow and the green of Downpatrick was exhilarating, and Harry and Juana happily settled amongst a friendly and generous people. In the neighbourhood were a number of discharged soldiers for whom Harry had a natural affinity, including one old boy who was apt to get drunk on anniversaries of battles, but more recently on a regular daily basis. When Harry remonstrated with him, he responded that there were so many anniversaries that he was frightened of missing one, so celebrated just in case.

The stay in Ireland was relatively brief for Harry and Juana as he was ordered to leave for Halifax, Nova Scotia, in September, in command of two and a half companies of his Regiment. Now thirty-seven, Harry was very pleased on arrival in Nova Scotia to find his former Brigade Commander, Sir James Kempt, to be the Governor. Not only that, there were troops there, mainly of the 52nd, old cronies of the 95th, who remembered Harry and Juana from Bordeaux in 1814, and enquired after her horse and dog with affection. The Smiths thoroughly enjoyed Nova Scotia, with regattas, horse racing, picnics and amateur theatricals, despite Harry having to revert to the half-pay of an unattached major (i.e. not within his Regiment), although he had been in temporary command of the Battalion. Sir James Kempt took him on as his ADC and Harry learned much about the administration of government, which was to stand him in good stead later on.

In November, Harry and Juana were on the move again, this time to Jamaica, where Harry was to assume the appointment of Deputy Quartermaster General in the rank of Lieutenant Colonel. His departure from Canada was marked by an extraordinary outpouring of affection from troops he was unlikely ever to serve with again – he and they knew it, thus making their farewells even more poignant. He was chaired, shoulder high, by officers and soldiers, to the ship to take him and Juana to Jamaica. Little boats followed them to the entrance to the harbour, then they were alone, parted from their faithful old friends, veteran comrades and what Harry described as three of the most renowned regiments of the Duke's old army.

Twenty-eight days later they arrived at Kingston, Jamaica, and soon after they had landed, the entire crew of the ship, bar the old German carpenter, died of yellow fever, an unpleasant foretaste of things to come.

Harry's job was to sort out some pretty poor administration. He set to with his usual drive and found that one barracks, because it was a Royal Establishment, was perfectly acceptable; others, because they were merely Colonial Establishments, were a disgrace. The soldier's 'bed' was just a blanket, the very feel of which, in a tropical climate, was unpleasant, and was merely laid on the floor. A submission was promptly put to Horse Guards in London where the Duke of Wellington was

Commander-in-Chief, and within a few months, every soldier had a proper bed, with sheets etc.

The real scourge was yellow fever, a serious viral infection transmitted by mosquitoes in tropical regions. In mild cases the symptoms are similar to influenza, but serious cases develop a high temperature and may have a series of after-effects, such as internal bleeding, kidney failure and meningitis. A classic feature of yellow fever is hepatitis, which is the reason for the yellow colouring of the skin (jaundice) and hence the name of the disease. Yellow fever can cause sudden epidemics, with a mortality rate of almost 50 per cent. Mainly brought in by sailors, it quickly spread amongst the regiments on the Island. In six weeks, twenty-two officers and 668 soldiers died. With the Governor up-country, Harry had to tackle the problem himself. In consultation with the Chief Medical Officer, he moved the 84th out of their barracks to a bivouac camp in the countryside. This had the desired effect, sickness went down and morale returned. Harry and Juana were tireless in their efforts to combat this terrible disease. Never sparing themselves, they would ride 35 miles a day, and often a further 15 in an open boat, visiting, helping and encouraging despondent soldiers. Despite opposition and difficulties, Harry established convalescent accommodation where sick men could recover properly before returning to their units. Gradually, the epidemic came under control and twelve months after Harry had moved the sickly 84th to their bivouac site, they were inspected by the Governor. This time, not a man was in hospital and the only soldier not in the ranks was standing in the rear as he had a fractured leg.

Harry and Juana made a tour of the Island with the Governor, the latter by boat and Harry and Juana by open coach, meeting up at some grand colonial mansion each night. Highly conscious of the iniquities of the slave trade, Harry was gratified to see slave conditions had improved. Slaves were better looked after than many peasants he had seen in other parts of the world – they were happier, better fed, less hard worked, had better medical facilities, better education and, indeed, provision was even made for old age. Many lived in little huts with their own gardens. He sometimes felt, ruefully, that they were better off than his soldiers.

Harry and Juana found an idyllic spot in the mountains where they were above the extreme heat of the plains and rainfall was sufficient to make everything grow well. He visited his low-lying office only twice a week. But this halcyon existence was to be brought to an abrupt end when a note arrived from Lord Fitzroy Somerset to the effect that the C-in-C was so pleased with his performance in Jamaica, he was now appointing Harry to be Deputy Quartermaster General in the Cape of Good Hope. With forty-eight hours notice, Harry and Juana were aboard ship and bound for the Colony, but first via England for a brief reunion with the family before taking up the post. So once again they were entering another, totally different, chapter of their lives, this time to the unknown south of the Dark Continent. Once they left England, they were not to return until 1847.

## Chapter 6

# The Cape and Frontier Wars January 1829 to June 1840

In the years after 1815, it appeared that wherever Harry and Juana went they met old friends who, like themselves, were Peninsula veterans. In 1829, after a delightful voyage of only eleven weeks – shorter than expected – they arrived in Table Bay. John Bell, an old friend, welcomed them warmly and insisted that, initially, they stay at his house. Juana was delighted with the affectionate welcome and the pleasant sunshine, a change from the bleak winds of Nova Scotia and the steamy heat of Jamaica. The day after they arrived, Harry rode out to see the Governor, Sir Lowry Cole, another old friend who had commanded the 4th Division in the Peninsula. Cole explained that Harry would be Commandant of the Garrison, in addition to being Deputy Quartermaster General, a position second only to the Governor.

Harry realized that he would now face civil as well as military problems and set out to learn as much as possible about the wider issues facing the Government. The British Navy's control of the sea had played a significant role in supplying Wellington's forces through Lisbon and Harry had already been involved in their escapades in South America. Now he found their role in Cape Colony was equally significant. As Napoleon overran the countries of Europe, Britain, with its naval dominance, used the opportunity to annex their colonial possessions. The Dutch had settled Cape Colony and in 1805, after a brief skirmish at Blauwberg, it was taken over by the British. At first all seemed well, and the pastoralist and paternalist Dutch settlers quietly continued their lives. They held to the puritanical views of the Dutch Reformed Church, which were directly linked to a life based on cattle farming and the use of slaves. But gradually, British policy, which established English as the official language and used British law, and aggressive attacks by powerful missionary groups, seemed to the Boers to threaten their language, their religion and their way of life.

In Cape Town, there was always a clash of interest between the city dwellers, the farmers and adventurers who eagerly expanded the frontier to the east and north, and the missionaries, who stoutly defended the rights of the native tribes, especially the Hottentots and Griquas in the remote frontier areas. The frontier (see map on page 160) and its problems were to occupy the lives of Harry and Juana for many years. From 1820 onwards, Britain encouraged large numbers of its people to settle in the eastern Cape, and this increased the demand for expansion into what many considered, incorrectly, to be the empty lands of the veldt. The frontier lands were far from empty and in the 1820s were under intense pressure from the so-called Bantu. These were African people often fleeing southwards from the depredations of the Zulu nation under their formidable military leader Shaka, then at the height of his powers. Operating over a wide area around present-day Durban, Shaka, with his original military ideas, established Zulu military power at such a level that decades later the Zulus could challenge the British at Isandlwana and Rorke's Drift. Much of Harry's effort and many of his dramatic rides, sometimes accompanied by Juana, related to the expanding frontier and the Bantu issue.

After they had settled into their home in Cape Town, Harry thought 'no man was ever more happily placed'. He and Juana lived in a delightful house some distance from the Governor's residence, with 'capital stables'; the garrison he commanded consisted of an artillery battery and a battalion of the 72nd Regiment (later the Seaforth Highlanders). He set to work to reorganize unnecessary guards and duties, gaining an admirable response from the troops. He abolished the guard of eight soldiers at the Observatory, remarking that the stargazers found that they could carry on 'their celestial pursuits without the aid of terrestrial soldiers'. He trained all the troops up to the exacting standards of the Light Bobs and carried out exercises with live ammunition without a single casualty. Soon afterwards, Lord Dalhousie, who had been with Harry at the Battle of Vitoria and again in America, called at the Cape on his way to India as Commander-in-Chief, and Harry staged a mock battle with his newly trained troops. As Deputy Quartermaster General in the Colony, Harry was the senior military officer with administrative, discipline and quartermaster responsibilities.

Hunting and shooting were never far from Harry's thoughts and he was able to indulge his passion enthusiastically. High-quality horses from thoroughbred English stock gave him ample choice and soon he had an excellent stud. Around Cape Town, hunting had an added hazard because moles the size of rabbits made deep holes, which in wet weather were highly dangerous to horses and caused damaging falls. After describing the excitement of hunting antelope with his horses and an excellent pack of hounds, he added that further away near the frontier was the fleetest deer of all – the springbok.

During the shooting season, Harry and Juana used to go off to visit a retired officer of the 21st Dragoons, who was farming some miles away and whose land provided very good partridge and grouse shooting. A huge wagon, drawn by eight horses, took all their gear, and was accompanied by greyhounds, pointers, terriers and spaniels. Harry concluded his description of hunting and shooting by adding that he and Juana enjoyed this life, which was full of kindness, hospitality and happiness, from soon after their arrival until 1834. During that time their friend Sir Lowry Cole retired and was succeeded as Governor and Commander-in-Chief by Sir Benjamin D'Urban.

Soon after the arrival of D'Urban as Governor, there was a serious outbreak among the Kaffir tribes on the frontier. Harry described this outbreak as 'An irresistible rush, carrying with them fire, sword, devastation and cold-blooded murder, and spoiling the fertile estates and farms like a mountain avalanche'. The centre of the outbreak lay some 600 miles east of Cape Town, and D'Urban sent Harry to deal with it by all necessary means. A naval sloop was ready to take him, but, mindful of the frustrating days they waited at Harwich before Waterloo, Harry decided to ride to Grahamstown. Post horses were arranged for a seven-day ride, and at the same time half of 72nd Regiment was sent by sea and half by wagon. D'Urban gave Harry clear instructions and promised to support him in every way.

On 1 January 1835, Harry, with one servant, set off before daybreak on a 90-mile ride for the first day – with the heat raging like a furnace. He carried important documents, which Juana had sewn into the lining of his jacket. In spite of a severe thunderstorm he reached his first stop by late afternoon. The next day, he again rode for nearly 90 miles on a game little horse which impressed him so much he decided to buy it. On the third day he planned to ride a hundred miles, but it proved to be a day of frustration. At one stage no horses were ready and at the next town a great dinner had been prepared, which he had to stop and eat, and from which he suffered for the rest of the day. Then more frustration at the next town where there was a civic reception, which delayed him still further. The following day he intercepted mail from Grahamstown which included dire reports of disasters and murders, and the fear that Grahamstown would have to be abandoned. At this news he sent messages ahead to have his horses ready a day early. Throughout this ride he suffered from intense heat and the next day, after his horse had collapsed, a Dutch farmer refused to lend him a horse so Harry knocked him out, jumped on the horse and rode off. On the last day of the journey, having ridden 'wretched knocked up horses', he was met by an escort of Cape Mounted Rifles, given a good horse and so at last reached Grahamstown – only to be faced by another civic reception and another huge dinner. As he approached the town, he found an atmosphere of complete panic, and passed families fleeing with their herds and all their possessions. Much of the detail of this remarkable expedition is given in his affectionate letters to Juana – *mi queridissima muger* – my dearest wife.

In Grahamstown he found fear, panic, chaos and confusion, with ineffective barricades, and everyone heavily armed and liable to shoot each other. Harry, with his memories of Badajoz, tried not to laugh. He went to Colonel Somerset's house, gave orders, demanded the necessary documents by daybreak, and said he would establish martial law in the morning. Several outlying posts had been abandoned and some missionaries were in peril, besieged in a settlement a few miles away. After martial law was established, a Dutch burgher was objectionable, so

Harry put him in jail and took over his house. He ordered the immediate creation of a Corp of Volunteers, and then in a meeting of excited and terrified burghers, he decided to take over and assert his authority. He asked why his orders had not been carried out, and when the chairman started arguing, Harry, in a voice of thunder, said that anyone who did not instantly obey his orders would be court-martialled and punished. He quickly established control, organized the Volunteers, and showed that defence consisted of military vigilance and not cowering behind barricades inside your own house.

The next day, Harry organized a force of 300 men, under an experienced Rifles officer, to attack the kraal of a local Kaffir chief who was the leader of the uprising, and whom Harry described as 'a double faced old murderer and breaker of treaties'. The chief narrowly escaped, but the effect of the attack was dramatic and the forces of the Kaffir uprising withdrew from the immediate area. When the 72nd Regiment arrived, they quickly recaptured an outlying fort. Next, a Rifles officer led a swift attack and rescued the missionaries, who had daily expected to have their throats cut. Harry thought that the rescue of the missionaries was one of the best single things he did in the Kaffir War, but the missionaries never acknowledged it and were always ready to censure – as Harry was later to find out. The day after the rescue, the Governor arrived and issued a special General Order commending the outstanding achievement of Colonel Smith, which was beyond all praise and deserving the gratitude of the whole Colony.

D'Urban confirmed and extended Harry's powers so that he could deal effectively with all the problems of the area. He quickly organized four companies – each about 100 strong – from the Hottentots, the original native people of the Cape, and found that they quickly became good soldiers. Harry stayed several weeks, campaigning in the area of Grahamstown and up to the Fish River and beyond. His forces captured thousands of cattle, some which had been stolen and some the property of the revolting Kaffirs, finding that this was an effective way of hitting at the enemy. Even with all this hectic activity he wrote to Juana almost every day and on 7 April he reminded her that it was the twenty-third anniversary of the dramatic moment in Badajoz when they had first seen each other. He opened his letter with *'mi queridissima ma muger'*, my dearest wife, and at the end wrote: 'God bless you old woman, and do not be afraid, God will take care of us.'

The news of the revolt on the frontier had arrived when Harry and Juana were at the Governor's New Year's Eve party, and D'Urban had instantly discussed it with Harry. When, almost immediately afterwards, he galloped off on his famous ride, he and Juana did not realize that they were in for a long separation. Their home, 'a dear little cottage in Rondesbosch', though substantially larger than the family house in Whittlesey, provided Juana with a safe and secure base for a happy and active social life while Harry was away. She was surrounded by a number of old friends, including the Lowry Coles and their large family, she was active in community activities and she regularly taught in a school for African girls. Cape Town was growing rapidly and could already boast a public library of 30,000 volumes. There seemed to be an almost constant stream of visitors from the ships bound for India, the Far East and Australia, which called in at the Cape for a welcome break from their long voyages. Many of these, once again, were old Peninsula friends, often going to fairly senior appointments in the army or the civil administration in India. For Juana and Harry, thoughts of their future often turned to India, where numerous campaigns brought the possibility of promotion. The main hotel, St George's, relied substantially on the Indian passing trade and it was here that Juana was frequently entertained. Visitors usually brought eagerly awaited news from London and especially the latest news from Parliament about the slavery issue. Just occasionally a visitor called in after doing the unutterably tedious garrison duty on St Helena.

During this period of separation, Juana finally decided to join the Church of England which brought deep satisfaction for Harry although, in consequence, she was disowned by her remaining Spanish relatives. As their separation dragged on, Juana constantly begged to come and join Harry. She reminded him of her long months of campaigning in Spain, when she had never complained. Every letter from Harry reassured her of his deep and constant love, but never said a word about her joining him. There was some slight solace when he suggested that she started to write down details of all their adventures together, remarking light-heartedly that one day it might be published as Harry and Jenny Smith. She attended social functions, including balls in Government House, no longer the dazzling young wife but a rather plump Spanish matron, albeit splendidly attired. But still her thoughts were on the frontier with Harry.

By early 1835, having pacified the area around Grahamstown and the Great Fish River, Harry had to tackle the bigger problem of the powerful chief Hintza, who controlled a vast territory up to and beyond the River Kei, some hundred miles beyond Grahamstown. Hintza and his forces had caused havoc along the frontier, frequently clashing with Dutch trekkers who were moving into the area. Harry reflected uncritically the view of the British as they moved into many parts of Africa, that they were bringing law and order and the benefits of civilization to a dark continent. It did not occur to the supporters of British expansion that Hintza and many others were defending their lands against attack by alien intruders. After reports that Hintza's men had made ferocious attacks on mission stations and had stolen thousands of cattle, Harry marched his forces beyond the River Kei to a mission station deep into Hintza's territory. For weeks the British had made overtures to Hintza to arrange a peaceful settlement, but constantly received evasive answers.

Harry led a strong force, including his faithful Scottish Highlanders, some Hottentot units and also new units of Fingoes, a tribe which Hintza had cowed into slavery. As the British advanced, Hintza's chief representative came to the headquarters. Harry described him as 'a sharp wolf-like fellow with the cunning of Satan'. After lengthy and patient discussion it became clear that Hintza had not the slightest intention of restoring the cattle he had stolen or making restitution for destroying the mission station, and D'Urban, who had now joined Harry, therefore formally declared war. On 24 April 1835, Harry moved his forces, including some cavalry, further into Hintza's country. While his main force advanced, Harry, really in his element, led fighting patrols against Hintza's different kraals and rounded up thousands of cattle which had been stolen from the settlers. Then, in a rapid manoeuvre, he led the attack on Hintza's main kraal. Hintza had fled but in a significant gesture his whole kraal was burned down. Hintza had treated every previous approach with contempt, but the burning of his kraal had a dramatic effect. Almost immediately he came into the British camp with a group of followers to make peace with the Governor. D'Urban formally read out all the charges against him and he asked to have until the next day to consider the situation. Harry made certain that his prisoner was very carefully guarded, but during the evening they had a formal dinner during which a bullock was ceremonially slaughtered – described by Harry in gruesome detail in his autobiography.

The following day a formal court was set up, presided over with due pomp by D'Urban, and peace was officially proclaimed. Hintza, appearing to cooperate, agreed to send messages to all his chiefs with orders to them to bring in their quota of cattle. In the meantime, he remained in Harry's HQ virtually as a prisoner. During the peace negotiations, Hintza's forces started to attack the Fingoes, but they desisted when Harry threatened to hang Hintza, his brother and his son. Soon afterwards, an elderly representative of Hintza came into Harry's HQ and it was later discovered that Hintza had sent him in order to murder Harry. D'Urban distrusted Hintza from the start, but he did allow Harry, with a strong military force, to take the chief back to his lands to collect the stolen cattle. When Hintza asked what his position was Harry replied that he was a prisoner, and if he tried to escape he would be shot. They travelled for several days and Hintza often behaved suspiciously. Then, when they were close to a deep valley and close to several Kaffir villages, Hintza tried to escape. He spurred his horse away, but Harry galloped after him and after a desperate ride, managed to pull Hintza off his horse. Before Harry could turn his horse round Hintza had disappeared into the thick bush. The military escort quickly spread out and in the ensuing melee, confusion and darkness, Hintza was shot.

On the frontier, D'Urban and Harry faced a complex situation. On the one hand, their handling of the general unrest and especially their treatment of Hintza was seriously criticized by the missionaries, who had powerful contacts back in London at Exeter Hall, the headquarters of evangelical and missionary activity. On the other, they fell foul of the Boer settlers for being far too lenient with Hintza and his warriors who had spread murder and mayhem across the whole area. The Hintza crisis drew D'Urban and Harry together, although there is evidence of some disagreement. Harry criticized D'Urban for being too cautious and dilatory, and D'Urban, in a personal letter, pointed out that because of Harry's hasty and impetuous actions, there were fairly serious doubts about putting real power into his hands.

In his autobiography, Harry described very briefly how Hintza, in attempting to escape, was shot. He did not realize at the time the very serious implications this incident would have. Glenelg, the Colonial Secretary, who was strongly influenced by the evangelical lobby, not only criticized the forward policy on the frontier, but, after receiving an independent report, demanded a Court of Inquiry into the death of Hintza. The report alleged that in his attempt to escape, Hintza had been wounded and then had been shot in cold blood. For Harry, the Inquiry was both humiliating and frustrating, and in its final statement it was critical of his description of Hintza's death. The intensity of their feelings is illustrated in the personal letters between D'Urban and Harry. D'Urban wrote that Glenelg's ravings were fanatic and imbecile, and Harry reacted furiously at the canting hypocrisy of philanthropists and 'their damned Jesuitical procedures'. In a letter to Glenelg, Harry bitterly regretted that he had believed the 'trumped up fabrications of a double-faced scoundrel'. Although Glenelg subsequently apologized, his actions caused grave hurt to Harry and damage to his reputation. Allegations and recriminations about the death of Hintza have continued into the twenty-first century.

On the ground, immediately after Hintza's death, Harry's force was in serious danger, because Hintza had led them into his stronghold, and the news of his death could well rouse his people to fury. Harry gathered his units together, urged their total vigilance and quickly moved off. They covered 80 miles in three days, but he kept them going and set off at 3.00am, leaving only 'jaded horses and weakly men' under an experienced Peninsula officer as a guard on the cattle they had recovered. As he had half expected, the Kaffirs did attack during the next night and murdered one section of the guards. Still in serious danger from large bodies of the enemy, Harry concentrated all his forces, set out strong defences with covering fire and prepared for another attack. On leaving this difficult and dangerous position, the British had to cross a deep, wooded river valley, but thanks to Harry's clear orders and positive leadership this was achieved without loss. He considered that it was the most dangerous situation he had ever been in. He described the handful of his people 'compared with the thousands of brawny savages all round us, screeching their war-cry, calling to their cattle, and indicating by gesticulations the pleasure they would have in cutting our throats'.

By the middle of May 1835, Harry and his troops were ready to fight their way forward, and they moved slowly westwards with 3,000 cattle which had been recovered, together with about 1,000 Fingoes who flocked to the British units for protection from their Hintza attackers. They had to cross very difficult mountainous country with deep valleys and fast-flowing rivers, but they safely rejoined the main force under D'Urban on 21 May. The Governor issued a special order praising the military skill and indefatigable activity of Colonel Smith and 'the admirable zeal, discipline and determined spirit' of his troops. He also praised the rescue of the Fingoes and the recovery of thousands of cattle.

During the campaign, Harry's letters to Juana give a vivid account of all his actions, together with discreet comments when D'Urban was present. In February, when the Governor arrived, Harry had written: 'Master is always floundering in the midst of information, whilst I like to take a look at the ground, march and take possession.' Despite this criticism, Harry came to revere D'Urban. Whatever pressures Harry was under, one thing always shone through his letters: 'The sum total of all my love, affection, regard, esteem, everything that is dear, to you alma mia'. In another letter he describes a hut which was built for him, but he wished his dear wife was in it. He gave amusing anecdotes of how he tried to cope with Dutch for the burghers and a few phrases for the Kaffirs. He showed his vigorous and cheerful personality which dominated the atmosphere of the camp. Two of his young officers, 'the impudent rascals', planned Fort Harry, and even drew a sketch of it. On another day, to please Harry, they drew Fort Wellington.

Harry's brisk and successful campaign, so warmly commended by D'Urban, had pacified a large area and saw the creation of Queen Adelaide Province, from the Fish River to the River Kei, with King

William's Town as the capital. Before he left for Cape Town, the Governor appointed Harry in full charge of the new province. This made it possible for him to write to Juana to say she could join him. Her journey was quickly planned. She would leave on 4 June, reach Fort Willshire by 23 June and be reunited with Harry the following day.

Harry – frequently with Juana by his side – threw himself into the arduous task of pacifying and civilizing the new province. He took a very strong line with the remaining Kaffir rebels and made it clear that above all he wanted to establish peace, but if they attacked him he would destroy them. It was still a dangerous situation and soon after Juana arrived a patrol, warned to be vigilant, and led by an experienced British officer, was completely wiped out without a shot being fired. In their growing headquarters, at first Harry and Juana had to sleep under canvas because their house was not ready, and they had to be protected by numerous sentries because of the danger of Kaffir attacks. The fairly large Fingo contingent, which Harry had rescued from Hintza's attacks, were now confident enough to drive off the Kaffirs from the headquarters area. Harry, helped greatly by Juana, tried to influence Kaffir women to curb their men's brutal and warlike tendencies, and to assist in the establishment of peace. After a long and determined effort, peace was at last established – in September 1835, D'Urban came to Fort Cox, halfway between Grahamstown and Fort Willshire, and formally agreed peace terms with Kreili, the son of Hintza.

After this, Harry and Juana started on the difficult but rewarding task of establishing law and order and civilized standards across the new province. Realizing that the chiefs wielded immense power, he appointed them as magistrates, and as a symbol of their authority issued them with a black cane with a brass knob. He ostentatiously used a very large cane and a bigger brass knob to show that the authority came from him. He called his HQ his 'Great Kraal' and encouraged all chiefs to send a representative to stay there to ensure good communication – only partly as a hostage. He appointed army officers to act as magistrates alongside the more important chiefs. This regime which he set up was remarkably similar to the system of Indirect Rule, which was used across most British colonial territories in Africa, from the time of Lord Lugard in 1900 until after the Second World War.

Harry discovered that a chief would frequently be in league with a powerful witch doctor, together creating an absolute tyranny over their people. The charge of witchcraft, which they frequently levied against an innocent man, especially if he owned many cattle, led to almost certain death, after horrifying torture – like tying a man to a stake in the ground and covering him with black ants. In spite of his best efforts, Harry discovered chiefs who still inflicted brutal punishments on their victims. He therefore called great meetings of chiefs with their people, and where necessary would publicly punish the chief who had broken the rules.

At the same time as gradually removing barbaric practices, he positively introduced the benefits of civilization. Key men in each tribe were taught to use oxen for ploughing and were encouraged to spread the practice. Trade slowly replaced barter and the use of money spread to most areas. Juana played an active part in the civilizing schemes by maintaining close contact with the wives of the chiefs, encouraging them to forward the civilizing process and the eradication of warlike and barbaric customs. Not quite the Lysistrata of Aristophanes, but along the same lines! Her influence was particularly significant when Harry attempted, successfully, to put a stop to the annual custom of a chief and his cronies having their way with all the young maidens of the tribe. Belief in magic remained a huge problem and Harry persevered in undermining it. In a special large gathering of chiefs and people, Harry brought in a chief who had been particularly truculent, and set out to prove that his magic was stronger. He had the engineers place on old wagon on the skyline and fill it with explosive. Then, before the assembled crowd, he stated that his magic was so powerful that he could merely point at a distant object and it would blow up. Which of course it did. Harry admired the very handsome physique of the African men and women, 'figures and eyes beyond conception', but surprisingly he seemed really offended by their nakedness and did his best to encourage them to wear clothes, normally animal skins. At the same time, while he hesitated to oppose polygamy, he did oppose the purchase of wives – usually nubile young maidens. He and Juana had some success in getting the families to oppose this practice.

They had thrown themselves heart and soul into the challenging but rewarding task of bringing peace and prosperity to the new province, when suddenly they were stopped in their tracks. The missionary lobby, the combative Reverend John Philip and the scheming Captain Stockenstrom, through their evangelical contacts in London, had prevailed on the vacillating Lord Glenelg, the Colonial Secretary, to remove Harry from his position, replace him by Stockenstrom, abandon Queen Adelaide Province, and withdraw British control back to the Fish River. Harry reacted furiously, writing years later that he remained deeply hurt and offended by the fierce criticism he received in the press. He wrote:

> The most crooked policy ever invented by the most wicked Machiavellians blasted all my hopes for the benefit of the barbarians committed to my rule, and the bright prospect of peace and tranquillity for the Colony ... it restored the province to barbarism, shook off the allegiance of the Kaffirs, and re-established the full plenitude of their barbarity ... I did not expect to be called a bloodthirsty murderer in every print in every quarter of our dominions or to be shamefully abandoned by the Minister of the Colonies.

He added that Stockenstrom was violently obnoxious to both the colonists and the Kaffirs. Harry was not likely to accept, without protest, such a calamity and the shattering of all his hopes for civilizing the province. He wrote to Glenelg with a full and lengthy justification of all his actions. Glenelg did not respond to him personally, but much later, in May 1837, he did send a dispatch to D'Urban, indirectly admitting his error, and stating that he was delighted to express the acknowledgement of the Government to Colonel Smith, 'not only for his Military Services but for his zealous, humane and enlightened administration of the Civil Government of the Province'.

In King William's Town, the whole population was horrified at the dismissal of Harry and Juana, who had won their respect and affection for bringing peace, justice and prosperity to the region. The wives of the chiefs, weeping and lamenting, heaped their valuables onto Juana. Harry, despite his fury, did his best to hand over to Stockenstrom, and then they left. He wrote: 'I had laboured day and night, God alone knows how

I had laboured, and to be so unkindly treated by the minister of my country was galling to a soldier whose good name is his only hope in the world.' As they travelled towards Cape Town, at every town they passed, they received an overwhelming welcome, a formal dinner and public presentations. Harry had arranged a light wagon with swinging seats for Juana and they had a delightful journey, with Harry able to ride off and chase game or ostriches as they went along. At Grahamstown, the whole population came out to bid them farewell and thank them for bringing peace and prosperity – a stark contrast to the dire situation when Harry arrived after his famous ride, in January 1835, twenty-two months before. After their return to Cape Town, they were showered with gifts and presentation silver plate, and were honoured with formal ceremonies expressing gratitude and admiration. The Dutch burghers, the officers of the garrison, all the military units and almost all the civilian organizations expressed their feelings with warm and generous donations.

There were further repercussions. Harry's rapid occupation of Queen Adelaide Province and its swift abandonment by Glenelg prompted one of the major events in South African history. The Dutch burghers, already alienated by the imposition of British law and language, and by the abolition of slavery on which their way of life depended, decided that Glenelg's weak truckling to the missionaries was the last straw. They started the Great Trek in which, with all their families, cattle and all their possessions, they trekked north, beyond British control and eventually established two independent Boer republics – the Orange Free State and the Transvaal. This was to impinge on Harry's life again when he returned to the Cape as Governor.

Harry's curt dismissal by Glenelg as a result of the machinations of the missionary lobby in London could have been disastrous for his career, but once again he was to find that he had a powerful backer in Whitehall. Instead of ignominious dismissal, thanks to the intervention of the Duke of Wellington, Harry was appointed Adjutant General of the forces in India. Within just a few days, he and Juana had to dispose of most of their belongings and hurriedly embark for new adventures in India.

# Chapter 7

# India
# June 1840 to July 1847

Harry and Juana arrived in India in June 1840 to find the Army enmeshed in a disastrous war in Afghanistan. Although dying to get into action, Harry had to endure the intense frustration of being a senior staff officer, as the Adjutant General at the Commander-in-Chief's headquarters. Here he was responsible for manning, discipline and operational support of the army in India.

They had had a dramatic voyage from the Cape to Madras, enduring a three-day gale, with topmasts carried away and sails shredded. Harry described the ship – a year later to be burned in Mauritius – as a 'log in the water'. Ominously, the storm occurred over the anniversary of Waterloo and, with a soldier's superstition and a belief in a Divine Hand, a reading from the 91st Psalm saw them safely into harbour. Harry, however, lost one of his six horses and the others were substantially shaken and bruised. What Juana felt is not recorded, though clearly she was apprehensive of this new and dangerous land, rife with fever and disease.

When they reached Madras, they were warmly welcomed by an old friend, Dr Murray, the medical services Inspector General who was to die of fever some two years later in Upper Bengal. A swift and uneventful voyage round to Calcutta followed and here they were met by more old friends and acquaintances, some of whom they had last seen in South Africa, which had become what we would now call a 'Rest and Recuperation' (or R&R) centre away from the unhealthy Indian climate.

In Calcutta, Harry and Juana fell comfortably into the delightful family atmosphere of Lord Auckland, the Governor General, and his sisters. Auckland was a pleasant enough man but lacked drive and charisma. Harry thought him 'sensible but timid'. Others – more critical – thought him weak and prone to unscrupulous policies. Sir Jasper Nicolls, the Commander-in-Chief, and his daughters added to the welcome. Sadly, Nicolls's wife had died previously in Rome on her way home. Harry was initially very wary of his immediate superior. He thought Sir Jasper a hard and uncommunicative man but, as time went on, he realized that he had a warm heart, a sound businesslike brain and an honesty not always found in the East India Company. Nicolls was a professional soldier of considerable experience in South America and the Peninsula, having commanded the 59th of Foot (later the East Lancashire Regiment), but he was not particularly comfortable with Harry's hotheaded impetuosity. Juana, though, was enchanted to find herself the object of much warm affection from the Nicolls girls.

Harry had hoped to be given command of troops, but when that failed to materialize, he assumed his staff appointment with quiet resignation. 'I get on very well here with the public functionaries of all descriptions tho' they are odd fellows to deal with. But I have very much learned to restrain an impetuosity which never produces so favourable a result as moderation, for, if right, it frequently makes you wrong.' India at this time was a real opportunity for the professional soldier. There were reputations to be made, medals to be won, the possibility of prize money and considerable financial advantages. For instance, an officer serving in England, even in the most ordinary regiment, let alone the Cavalry and Guards, required a private income. In India an officer could comfortably live on his pay, employ a servant or two and run a couple of polo ponies with a 'syce' or groom. This favourable situation had been created by the combination of the power of the Royal Navy, together with the huge mass of both British and Indian troops maintained in India. British policies led to expansion in Burma and Singapore, and led to the Opium Wars in China – the opium trade producing a substantial part of India's revenue, and 40 per cent of its exports.

With the defeat of France, Britain's main potential foe was seen to be Russia, particularly with its ambitions set on the wealth of India and the classic, and only, invasion route to it through Afghanistan. In late 1840 and early the following year, it looked as though the Anglo-Indian Army had achieved a reasonable settlement in Afghanistan. Shah Shujah was made Amir by the British, the Army moved out of the fortified citadel in Kabul into conventional cantonments, a complete brigade started to withdraw to India, families were summoned and soldiers settled down to normal garrison life. Ominous signs, though, were becoming increasingly apparent: supply columns crossing the Khyber Pass were being constantly attacked; tribal revolt in northern Baluchistan made the region ungovernable; and Shah Shujah's writ barely extended outside the main towns – certainly not down to the Helmand River. Finally, command of the forces in Afghanistan devolved onto the incompetent and indecisive General Elphinstone – described by contemporaries as 'elderly, fat, gouty and nearly senile'. How could ineffective officers such as this be placed in positions of critical command? Harry, though, had a soft spot for Elphinstone, who had commanded a regiment during the years of the occupation of France between 1815 and 1818 when he and Juana were there.

In October 1841, a brigade, which was part of the force reduction, was heavily attacked while withdrawing, only reaching Jellalabad with difficulty and significant losses. Murder and mayhem broke out in Kabul, where Elphinstone dithered and the situation rapidly deteriorated. The beginning of the end came on 6 January 1842 when, with a supposed safe-conduct guarantee from the Afghan warlords, the British garrison of Kabul set out for India. As part of the agreement, all guns had to be left behind bar one horse artillery battery and three mountain guns. A number of hostages, including Elphinstone and the redoubtable Lady Florentia Sale, were forced to remain in Kabul. They were the lucky ones. Lady Sale remarkably managed to write a journal during her captivity. Imprisoned in three small rooms in an Afghan chief's compound, where luxuries such as tables and chairs were rare, she concealed pages of her diary in her clothing and later smuggled out instalments. While the European hostages certainly had the most unpleasant time – sleeping on the floor, eating greasy Afghan mutton and only being able to wash once a week – those Indians disabled by

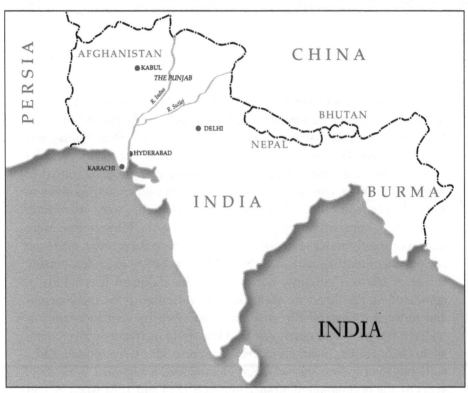

INDIA

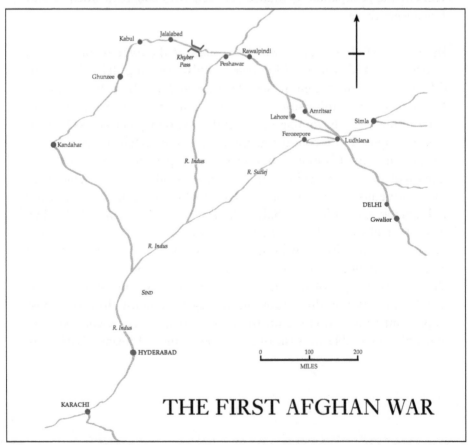

THE FIRST AFGHAN WAR

frostbite, or for whom rations were no longer available, were simply stripped of their clothes and possessions and pushed outside the compound to die. The withdrawing column was attacked the moment it left Kabul. Throughout the following days and freezing nights, the army was sniped at and duped with empty promises by the local tribesmen, in exchange for large sums of money. Further hostages were taken and the force subjected to continual local attacks and harassment. On the afternoon of 13 January, the single figure of Dr Brydon – immortalized in Lady Butler's iconic painting – approached Jellalabad on his exhausted horse. He was the sole European survivor, apart from the hostages, of a force of 690 British, 2,840 Indian soldiers and 12,000 camp followers. The 44th of Foot (later the Essex Regiment) lost twenty-two officers and 645 men. The shock wave was to be felt throughout the Empire.

Harry was beside himself with anger and frustration, constantly badgering the Commander-in-Chief, Sir Jasper Nicolls, to send him to Afghanistan. His view was that a strong and well-equipped force, moving fast, under decisive leadership – his, of course – would restore the situation. Nicolls, however, knew his Harry well and being of a less aggressive nature, clearly worried that, if put in charge, the only obstacle preventing him reaching Persia would be the Caspian Sea. Nicolls was not prepared to take the risk and wrote to Harry: 'Your rapid style has often made me think you were inclined, in your Peninsula manner, to take me by storm or surprise.' This professional disagreement did not, however, affect the very warm personal relationship that the Smiths had with the Nicolls family. Juana stayed with them when she was recovering from a tropical fever inevitably picked up in India, and they were very affectionate towards her.

Harry maintained that the depleted brigade in Jellalabad should have been swiftly reinforced and then the Afghans in Kabul attacked. As always, timing was crucial and the opportunity was soon lost, to Harry's increased fury. Furthermore, the so-called Army of Retribution, later sent into Afghanistan to avenge the disaster, instead of being given to Harry was split into two, with Brigadier Nott commanding in the south and General Pollock in the north. They were both junior to Harry. He sarcastically compared the bickering between the two to Napoleon's quarrelling Marshals in Spain. Nevertheless, in March 1842, Pollock's force arrived at Jellalabad to find that the garrison had courageously beaten off the besieging Afghans. This was a major fillip to British morale in India and when the 13th of Foot (later the Somerset Light Infantry) marched back to India out of Jellalabad, every garrison the Battalion went through gave them a ten-gun salute. From then on the Regiment wore, as part of their cap badge, a depiction of the walls of the town, with the word 'Jellalabad' superimposed. In the south, Nott resolutely held Kandahar with a well-trained force.

In the meantime, Lord Ellenborough had replaced Lord Auckland as Governor General in Calcutta. Initially, on Ellenborough's arrival, Harry had thought he stood more chance of a command appointment, but this soon turned sour. Harry criticized Ellenborough, who he privately called 'The Moghul' for his fondness for pomp and ceremony, for having little idea of time, and for lack of foresight and the knowledge of preparations required to deploy a large army. Both Nott and Pollock confidently anticipated orders to free the hostages held in Kabul. To their astonishment they were initially ordered to retreat to India and, by implication, abandon Kabul to its fate. Harry was incensed and issued a number of Memoranda in August and September 1842. These went out on a widespread distribution and were not only highly critical of the strategy employed by his superiors but added his own views as to how the campaign should have been run. It is remarkable that, whether right or wrong, Harry escaped censure from the Commander-in-Chief for what amounted to insubordination or, at the very least, disloyalty. Perhaps it was realized that he was right.

The order to retreat was soon rescinded and both commanders were then given wide rein to withdraw to India, via Kabul. Pollock reached Kabul on 15 September, having extracted revenge on the way with the utmost severity. Nott made less progress from the south and had his force badly mauled by the Afghans at Ghunzee, but eventually arrived in Kabul on 17 September, infuriated to find Pollock there before him. The hostages were rescued some way from Kabul but, when found, had cleverly negotiated their own release. Elphinstone had died in captivity, so this was probably the work of the formidable Lady Florentia Sale.

(Lady Sale was one of the indomitable women of the Victorian Empire. Born Florentia Wynch, she was twenty-one when she married Captain Robert Sale, by whom she had twelve children, one of whom, Mrs Alexandrina Sturt, shared with her mother the horrors of the march from Kabul. Lady Sale was then fifty-four, but although she was twice wounded and had her clothing shot through, she worked tirelessly for the sick and wounded, and for the women and children who took part in that fearful journey. Throughout the march, and during the months which she suffered in Afghan captivity, she kept the diary, which exists to today. It is one of the great military journals and a remarkable personal memoir of a woman, who recorded battle, massacre, earthquake, hardship, escape and everyday detail with a sharp and often caustic eye. Her reaction when soldiers were reluctant to take up their muskets to form an advance guard was: 'You had better give me one, and I will lead the party.' Other typical observations are: 'I had, fortunately, only one ball in my arm,' and the brisk entry for 24 July, when she was a prisoner: 'At two p.m. Mrs. Sturt presented me with a grand-daughter – another female captive.' During the march her son-in-law, Captain Sturt, had died beside her in the snow. Her heroism was rewarded by an annual pension of £500 from Queen Victoria and when she died in her sixty-sixth year, her tombstone was given the appropriate inscription: 'Under this stone reposes all that could die of Lady Sale.')

Harry's view was that Nott and Pollock, being divided, were lucky to survive. Had the Afghans managed to consolidate their forces, always difficult in tribal communities, they would, undoubtedly, have taken Pollock and Nott apart piecemeal, but, as Harry rather smugly said, 'In all wars the folly of one party is exceeded by that of the other, and that which is least culpable succeeds.' On their withdrawal back to India, both forces set about destroying villages and towns, including Jellalabad, with the utmost ferocity while at the same time being harried by local tribesmen.

Ellenborough, who fancied himself as an orator, decided to welcome the avenging army back to Ferozepore in December 1842 with a dazzling display of elephants in gilded accoutrements, triumphal arches and numerous speeches. In the event it all turned to dust. The tired and dirty returning troops were drawn up in some sort of star formation, the arches tottered, the terrified elephants bolted and the Indian princes, whom all this was designed to impress, thought the whole thing a joke. So instead of consolidating British prestige and power in India, loss of face and status started to sow dangerous seeds of rebellion and ridicule. The British experience in the First Afghan War was destructive and dramatic, and, sensibly, they kept out of Afghanistan for another thirty years. How would those involved then have commiserated with today's British soldiers, still fighting much the same people over the same territory?

At this time, successive British governors were determined to keep the Indus valley open for trade and as an important route from the port of Karachi up to the Punjab. In contrast, the Amirs of Sind were equally determined to prey on all the traffic passing through. This gave Ellenborough sufficient reason to prepare a large force and to order the aggressive General Charles Napier into the province to crush any resistance. He set about the task with severity and relish. (He was the elder brother of the less fiery George and William. Between the three of them they had sustained twenty-three wounds in the Peninsula.) By March 1843, Napier had subdued Sind and sent the famous message, probably apocryphal and later thought up by some clever classicist, 'Peccavi' ('I have sinned'). Harry was green with envy. If anyone was going to carry out this sort of operation, he thought, it should be him. This was compounded when Napier was made Governor of Sind Province, made Knight Grand Cross of the Order of the Bath (GCB) and given £50,000 as his share of the plunder. Harry sourly commented that that ended his financial worries, but Napier proved himself a resolute and efficient governor. He had to deal with a serious outbreak of Suttee – the custom of burning a widow on her husband's funeral pyre. When he was told that it was a national custom, he replied that we too had a national custom – that when men burn women alive, we hang them.

Although living in India was financially easier than England, Harry and Juana had considerable social responsibilities due to his position, and there was no such thing as an 'entertainment allowance'. Coupled with that, he was supporting his favourite sister, Alice (Mrs Sargant), and her two sons. He did receive £75 a year as Colonel of the 3rd Regiment of Foot (later The Buffs) but it did not go far. Prize money, without a command appointment, so far eluded him.

In July 1843, Sir Jasper Nicolls handed over command to Sir Hugh Gough. Harry had rather hoped his old friend Sir Benjamin D'Urban, with whom he had had such a close rapport in South Africa, would have been appointed, but it was not to be. Gough arrived with a sound reputation from the Peninsula and the Opium Wars and was known as a 'soldier's soldier' – an officer who looked after his troops and did not ask of them something he was not prepared to do himself. He wore a conspicuous white coat in battle in order to draw enemy fire onto himself rather than his troops (Wellington would not have approved). Despite their differences over Afghanistan, Harry and Juana parted from the Nicolls with a good deal of sadness. Juana and the Nicolls daughters clearly enjoyed each other's company and, although now aged forty-five, which by standards of the day was certainly middle-aged, Juana found them highly amusing. The Smiths then spent an unpleasant twelve days in the muggy heat of Calcutta, in the middle of the rainy season, welcoming the new Commander-in-Chief and being involved in endless briefings. As fellow 'front-line' soldiers, Gough and Harry had a natural affinity for each other. However, in the view of Harry and others, Gough was no military intellectual and his reaction to a threat was to take it head-on without much thought, let alone guile. This was to be, very nearly, his undoing in the 2nd Sikh War after Harry had left. However, the immediate problem facing the East India Company was trouble in Gwalior and the coordination of an army to deal with it.

The campaign in Gwalior, often called the 'One Day War' was the result of internal dissent and intrigue in the Maharatta court. The Court was riven with complex and dynastic feuds, and struggles for supremacy. Ellenborough happily followed the policy that the British had the right to intervene in the internal affairs of Indian States if they considered it was in the interests of peace and stability. The reality was that an unfriendly Gwalior – with its sizeable and ill-disciplined army – could threaten British lines of communication. If the Maharattas allied themselves to the Sikhs, though that was unlikely, British India could be in real trouble.

Ellenborough, the Governor General, and Gough, the Commander-in-Chief, were determined that the Maharattas should be in no doubt as to the power of the East India Company and the Queen Empress, either by force of arms in battle or by a significant demonstration of power. Harry, of course, still Adjutant General, was heavily involved in the planning and organization of a force of considerable strength. He was appalled how cumbersome and slow moving was such an army. The sheer size, with its siege equipment, bullock carts, elephants, camels and thousands of servants and camp followers, spread over a vast country with few roads, exasperated a man used to moving fast and lightly equipped. The rate of progress was little better than 2 miles an hour, with frequent halts to allow the baggage train to close up.

Gough crossed into the State of Gwalior, from Agra, with the main part of the army, while sending a division under General Grey to provide a distraction and divert the opposition from the south. On 26 December 1843, Gough invited the Maharatta leaders to meet him to negotiate, but they were so suspicious of Grey's divisional moves and upset by the violation of their territory that they were not prepared to attend.

Harry, far from sitting in the headquarters, went out on a reconnaissance patrol of his own. Having identified the position of an enemy force of about 10,000, he immediately reported to Gough. Grey's exact whereabouts were unknown and so Harry recommended that, as speed was essential to catch the enemy off guard, they should not wait for Grey but attack the enemy as soon as possible. They therefore set off before dawn the following day, 29 December, on an approach march of some 8 miles and attacked the enemy at Maharajpore, just outside Gwalior. Remarkably, they were accompanied by several of the officers' ladies, including Juana, mounted on elephants. Harry noted: 'Juana was under heavy cannonade with Lady Gough, Miss Gough, and a Mrs Curtis on their elephants. Juana had this command of Amazons, and, as she was experienced and they young, her command was anything but satisfactory.' Sir Charles Napier, writing in early 1844, could not resist pulling Harry's leg:

I congratulate you on your feats of arms. You had a tough job of it: these Asiatics hit hard, methinks. How came all the ladies to be in the fight? I suppose you all wanted to be gloriously rid of your wives? Well, there is something in that; but I wonder the women stand so atrocious an attempt. Poor things! I dare say they too had their hopes. They talk of our immoral conduct in Scinde! I am sure there never was any so bad as this. God forgive you all. Read your Bible, and wear your laurels.

In spite of Napier's disparaging remarks, Queen Victoria subsequently awarded Juana a special medal for her bravery when the elephants came under fire and she calmly took control.

The battle was a considerable success, though not without loss. Nearly half the 800 casualties were suffered by two British regiments, the 39th (later the Dorsets) and the 40th (later the South Lancashires), without whom, in Harry's view, the result might have gone the other way. The Maharattas fought hard and well, even firing horseshoes from their cannon when they ran out of ball. Harry had a narrow escape when a round bruised his foot, tearing off his stirrup leather and passing under his horse. His foot was numb for days. Peace was quickly concluded and the Maharatta army disbanded, but not before 10,000 men were enlisted into the British Army under European officers – the forerunners of many fine Sikh and Maharatta regiments which served with great distinction in the Indian Army until after the Second World War. Ellenborough, with his love of decorations, had medals made from captured cannon. Juana, having been as involved in the battle as anyone else, was also, properly, awarded the medal. Harry was so proud of his wife that he wrote to his sister, Alice, that he wanted her to have his jeweller make a gold star, as per his enclosed sketch, with enamel to represent the ribbon, which Juana could wear as a brooch. (This anticipated the diamond regimental badges of today that officers give their wives.) The two medals exist today (see plate section, photo 14). Interestingly, Harry also mentions his two nephews in the same letter. Hugh, son of Tom, was in Grey's Division and distinguished himself in their battle. Harry, Charles's son, was not so involved but reportedly conducted himself 'as cool as his usual placidity renders him'. Harry must have been very proud of them. He himself was Mentioned in

Dispatches and elevated from Companion of the Order of the Bath (CB) to Knight Commander (KCB). Probably even more satisfying for Harry was the personal letter from the Duke of Wellington, telling him of the award. Harry, understandably perhaps, could not fail to reply:

Headquarters, Army of India, Simla, 23rd June, 1844.

MY LORD DUKE,

I have this day had the honour to receive your Grace's letter, 'Horse Guards, 29th April,' acquainting me with an expression of satisfaction that Her Majesty had, upon your recommendation, been graciously pleased to appoint me a Knight Commander of the Most Honourable Military Order of the Bath. While my gratitude to my Sovereign is unbounded, my heart dictates, it is to your Grace I am indebted for every honorary distinction, promotion, and appointment I have received during a long and an eventful period of the history of the world.

Among the many thousands of the gallant soldiers who so nobly fought and conquered under your Grace, I may conscientiously hope none could desire more zealously to do his duty, or was ever more actuated by personal devotion or inspired with greater confidence throughout the numerous struggles of war, than he who now renders his grateful thanks for this mark of distinction so honourable to the soldier, and thus conferred by Her Majesty through the recommendation of his Commander-in-Chief, the Great Captain of the Age.

I have, etc.,

(Signed) H.G. SMITH.

Field Marshal His Grace the Duke of Wellington.

There now followed a relatively quiet time before the start of what, subsequently, came to be known as the First Sikh War in December 1845. The Sikhs of the Punjab, who lorded it over a poor and largely Muslim peasantry, were fiercely independent, having consistently resisted the Moghul kings in Delhi and the Muslims of Afghanistan. The charismatic ruler, Ranjit Singh, had, over the years, built up a powerful army. Its infantry were trained and modelled on European lines and their artillery, trained by French officers, was as good as any. Their weakness was the cavalry, which tended to be ill-disciplined and headstrong. With the death of Ranjit Singh in 1839, the ruling family in Lahore started to fall apart and was incapable of controlling the powerful army. There was intense intrigue, coupled with suspicions of treachery at Court, and they deeply distrusted the British, whom they had not allowed to cross their territory during the Afghan War. The British, in their turn, were highly suspicious of the Sikhs who made no secret of their ambitions to invade India. The army – the Khalsa – was difficult to deal with and some factions would have been happy to unleash it on the British; if it won, they would bask in its glory, if it lost, good riddance to a dangerous irritant. The smell of treason was never far away.

For Harry, with Juana in Simla, this was a time for serious reflection. He was, by now, a very seasoned soldier, both as a leader in the field and on the Staff. In the absence of any kind of Staff College or courses of instruction, he had learnt by experience. He had seen how the great leaders operated and behaved: Wellington, Picton, Craufurd, Moore and Beckwith. He had also observed the inadequacies and failures of Whitelocke, Leveson-Gower, Erskine, Dalrymple and the like. He tried, often successfully, to emulate the former and learn lessons from the latter. However, his experience was with physically hardened, highly disciplined and battle-inoculated troops of the Peninsula and Waterloo. Harry confessed India to be a different military scene altogether. No one seemed to give the enemy any credit for daring, dash and ability and, under Gough, the answer merely seemed to be a frontal assault with little finesse. Cooperation between the Arms – infantry, artillery and cavalry – was uncoordinated and Harry saw it as an unwieldy machine. Baggage trains were over-large, overextended and lacked proper administration. Soldiers frequently lacked basic equipment. Officers lacked real experience in handling Indian troops, and tactical intelligence on the enemy's strengths and weaknesses lay in the hands of a sprinkling of political officers and unreliable paid informers.

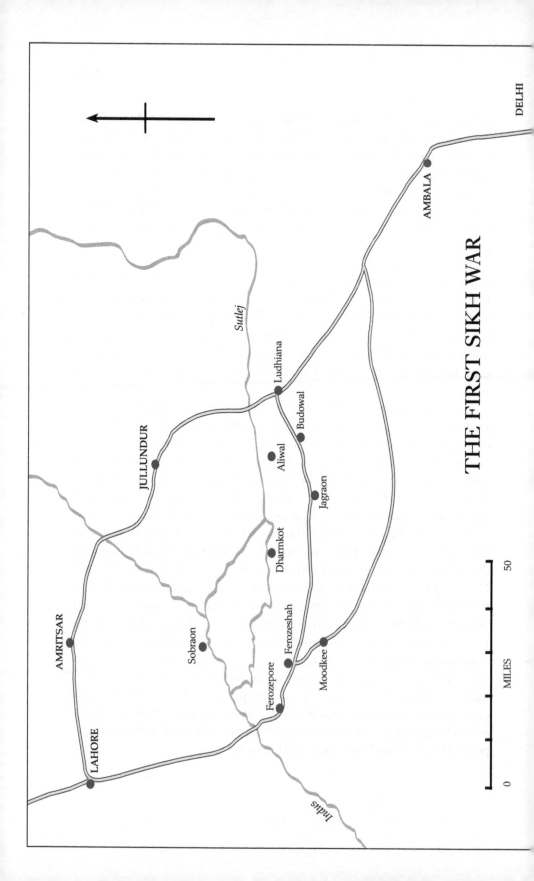

THE FIRST SIKH WAR

DELHI

AMBALA

Sutlej

Ludhiana

JULLUNDUR

Budowal

Aliwal

Jagraon

AMRITSAR

Dharmkot

Sobraon

Ferozeshah

Ferozepore

Moodkee

LAHORE

Indus

0        MILES        50

Maharajpore taught Harry a lesson he would never forget:

In this country almost every war has been terminated in one or two pitched battles fought as soon as the one army comes in sight of the other, and accordingly all the science attaching to advance and retreat, the posting of picquets, reconnaissance of the enemy, the daily contemplating of his movements, both when he is before you and on the march, are lost, and war is reduced at once to 'there are people drawn up who will shoot at you, so fire away at them.' You blindly and ineptly rush upon them, drive them from the field with considerable loss, take all their guns, and never see the vestige of them after. Thus we must judiciously and with foresight organize ourselves for a campaign in the Punjab – a very probable event – for the armies of India are not now the rabble they were in Clive's time, but organized and disciplined by European officers of experience (many French), and the art of war has progressed rapidly among our enemies, whose troops are invariably far more numerous than those we oppose to them; thus by superior ability we could alone calculate on their defeat. As it is, we calculate alone on the bulldog courage of Her Majesty's soldiers, and our loss becomes what we lately witnessed.

He urged that soldiers should be properly equipped with haversacks and water bottles (in one action, thirst was the major problem as the water-carriers had run away). He suggested proper training exercises, pitching one brigade against another, with blank ammunition, in the cold season. There was nothing wrong with the willingness or courage of the soldier, whether Indian or British, but as Harry neatly put it: 'the material is excellent … but now, like a dictionary, it contains all the words, but cannot write a letter.'

So while the British, for some time, anticipated a Sikh advance into India across the Sutlej River, they had made little practical preparation. Additionally, they were loath to expose their Sepoys to the Sikh propaganda of doubling the pay of anyone who fought for them. The British feared that even the smallest military reverse therefore could result in widespread desertion. Sikh commanders, however, for all their spirit, courage and daring, preferred to take up a position and wait to be attacked rather than developing the initiative themselves.

In 1844, Sir Henry Hardinge succeeded Lord Ellenborough as Governor General. He was a man of quality and ability with considerable military experience in the Peninsula, and he had lost his left hand at Waterloo. Seeing, quite rightly, that war with the Sikhs in the Punjab was inevitable, he began to have troops quietly moved northwest, and boats sent up the Indus and then onto the Sutlej to be prepared for pontooning. The isolated fortress of Ferozepore was reinforced with the task of watching the Sutlej river crossings and identifying any Sikh incursions.

By December 1845, all negotiations with the Sikhs had failed. Only Harry can explain the complexities:

> From the death of Runjeet Singh in 1839 to 1845 a succession of revolutions and murders of Kings and Princes continued, first one party, then another, supporting a reputed son of Runjeet on the throne, who was as sure to be murdered in the sanguinary struggles of that Reign of Terror. A Hill family, elevated for their personal beauty rather than their talents (although some of them were far from wanting abilities), became conspicuous, and many fell with the puppets of their creation. This family received the soubriquet of Lords of the Hills, Jummoo being the fortified hold of the head of the family. Its most conspicuous members were Goolab Singh and Dhyan Singh. Dhyan and his son Heera Singh were both Prime Ministers, or Wuzeer, and both were murdered in 1844. Such was the power of the standing army, it acknowledged no other authority, set up Kings and deposed them at pleasure, and at the period of the commencement of the war, a boy (Dhuleep Singh), born of a Hill woman of great ability and reputed the son of old Runjeet, was the nominal King, Lal Singh was Wuzeer, and Tej Singh Commander-in-Chief of this rabble (though highly organized and numerous) army. It must be obvious that such a state of things could not last. The resources of the treasury were rapidly consuming, and with them the only power of the Queen Mother, the Rani or Regent, which consisted in her presents and consequent popularity. All the foreign officers had absconded except one Frenchman, a man of neither note nor talent, and a Spanish Engineer by name Hubon, a low-bred man,

but clever, acute, and persevering. The British Government of India had acknowledged this Regency, and was desirous to retain amicable relationship with the Punjaub, but in the middle of the year 1845, so unruly and clamorous for war was the Sikh army, all negotiations terminated, and a state of uncertainty ensued which made it necessary for British India, without declaring hostility, to place itself on a footing to resist it, should so mad an enterprise ensue.

It was additionally rumoured that the Sikhs had already made plans, with a certain amount of local connivance, to place their Queen on the throne in Delhi. To Harry's amazement, a force reputed to be in the region of some 70,000 Sikhs managed to cross the Sutlej under the nose of Sir John Littler, commanding Ferozepore, and establish themselves in strength without Littler taking any action. With mounting anxiety, Gough pushed his Army towards the enemy by forced marches, reaching Moodkee on 18 December, but with the troops thoroughly exhausted and worn out. The Sikhs, meanwhile, had withdrawn to a position north-west of the town. By now, to his great satisfaction, Harry had been relieved of his Adjutant General's appointment and given command of the 1st Infantry Division. This proved to be the most important military appointment of his life, and he grasped the opportunity eagerly. Fearing the Sikhs would evaporate into the jungle, Gough ordered an immediate attack, despite the fatigue of his troops. The battle was straightforward, but hard fought. The British cavalry attacked both enemy flanks, leaving Harry's Infantry Division and a further two brigades to assault the centre. At one stage, when the 50th Foot (later the Royal West Kent Regiment) formed line to continue their advance from a square, Harry himself seized one of their Colours and led the charge with it. To everyone's relief, darkness brought an end to the battle and the Sikhs melted away. Gough's simple frontal attack caused substantial losses, including two major generals, McCaskill and Sale, the hero of Jellalabad and husband of Florentia. The Sikhs had fought well and, losing fewer troops than the British, lived to fight another day.

After the evacuation of the wounded and resupplying his Division, Harry prepared his troops for the next event, the battle for Ferozeshah, to which Lal Singh's Sikh force had withdrawn following Moodkee. The

Sikhs now occupied strongly fortified positions surrounding the town. Gough ordered the luckless General Littler in Ferozepore to leave the town, evade the Sikh blockade, and join forces with him before Ferozeshah. Characteristically, Gough was determined to attack the town without waiting for Littler's men. Luckily he was persuaded to wait by Sir Henry Hardinge who, although Governor General, had placed himself under Gough as his Second-in-Command. The assault began at 3.00pm, and with two hours of light left, Littler's troops led the attack from the left flank. Harry's Division was in reserve behind Hardinge and Gough. Immediately on contact, Littler's attack started to falter under the intense and accurate Sikh artillery fire and Harry pushed forward one of his brigades to reinforce them. Fierce fighting went on into the night, when Gough was forced to withdraw his forces from the town to pass the rest of the night as best they could amongst the casualties of the day's fighting, and still under sporadic Sikh fire. Harry himself was heavily involved, leading from the front, as was his custom. At the head of the 50th, he penetrated the heart of the enemy's position in the town and before dark had pushed through to the far side of it with a motley collection of troops. Moonlight, however, exposed the fragility of his unsupported position and the enemy rapidly closed in on him. At 3 o'clock in the morning, he found himself and his stragglers surrounded. Under a volley of covering fire, he managed to extract his troops and sought to rejoin Gough's force, leaving Ferozeshah on his left. Despite rumours of defeat and spurious orders to make his way to Ferozepore, Harry met up with Gough just before dawn. As the sun rose, to his chagrin, he could see, not 2 miles distant, the town he had just fought through so fiercely and escaped from so narrowly. Now, he was going to have to attack again.

The subsequent renewed attack was thoroughly successful. As the exhausted troops were, rightly, congratulating themselves, to their horror a fresh Sikh force from Ferozepore appeared. Almost out of ammunition, a horse artillery battery kept them at bay to allow time for Gough's forces to establish themselves into defensive positions. The Sikhs kept up a long artillery bombardment until, with a final heroic effort, Gough's cavalry put in a charge, forcing the enemy to abandon the field. By 4.00pm the battle was over. Gough could count himself lucky that the Sikh reinforcements had not pressed home their attack, which would have been almost impossible to resist given his troops' exhaustion and lack of ammunition. (To this day, the regiments involved hand over their Colours to the Sergeants' Mess on the anniversary of Ferozeshah, to commemorate the vital part played in the battle by sergeants.)

Gough now closed up to Ferozepore and regrouped, but was in no position yet to eliminate the Sikhs as a fighting force; he needed reinforcements to replace casualties and awaited the slow supply column, containing his heavy equipment, ponderously making its way from Delhi 200 miles to the south. The Sikhs, taking advantage of this inactivity and full of confidence, again crossed the Sutlej at Sobraon, with a force of some 8,000 troops and seventy guns, under Ranjodh Singh, to threaten the British base at Ludhiana and Gough's supply route.

Gough therefore dispatched Harry and his Division to counter the Sikh threat to Ludhiana and ultimately clear the incursion over the Sutlej. Typically, Harry wasted no time and set out two hours before dawn on 17 January 1846. Finding the small fort of Futteyghur unoccupied, he quickly moved on to Dharmkot just with his cavalry because the infantry were slowing him down. He gave the enemy garrison twenty minutes to consider their position. Wisely, they surrendered without an effective shot being fired. Gough then reinforced this success by providing Harry with the 16th Lancers and another battery of guns, and ordered him to proceed to Jagraon on the more southerly road, where he was to take under command the 53rd Foot (later the King's Own Shropshire Light Infantry). He was then to march the 25 miles to Ludhiana via Budowal. At Ludhiana he was to liaise with Colonel Godby who had four native regiments under him, including two Gurkha battalions, and four guns. Harry sent messages to Godby that he expected him to join his force halfway in order to put in a joint attack on the Sikhs. Harry left his slower moving baggage train under escort at Jograon and, in the early hours of 21 January, left to join Godby on the way to Ludhiana. After he had gone about 16-18 miles, he received word from Godby that further Sikh forces had arrived, giving them a total of around 10,000 troops and forty guns. He advised that their intention appeared to be to cut Harry's approach route from

Jagraon to Ludhiana, at Budowal. Godby stayed put. Harry invariably lavished praise where he thought it was due but he was, properly, intolerant of backsliders during the intensity of operations. On 25 January, he wrote to Gough: 'I send you Brigadier Gowran. I assure Your Excellency, I have no desire to retain him. I like young and spritely fellows who desire to overcome difficulties, not create them.'

Harry decided it was imperative to reach Ludhiana and take Godby's troops under command before he could deal with the current strength of the Sikhs. He therefore by-passed Budowal and reached Ludhiana by an indirect route, moving by night. Although subjected to sporadic attacks from the enemy, Harry's troops reached Ludhiana utterly exhausted, with foot soldiers being carried on horses behind cavalrymen, or hanging onto their stirrup leathers. The baggage train was less fortunate as it had been attacked throughout the day – many of the sick and wounded were butchered as they lay in litters and the greater part of the baggage looted. The soldiers hoped the Sikhs would drink the medicines thinking that they were wines. The 16th Lancers lost much of their regimental silver. (Years later, a lost silver cup turned up in a pawnshop in York. It was thought that it had been picked up by a camp follower and subsequently reached England.) To his fury, Harry's Waterloo medal was plundered and not replaced until 7 May that year (see plate section, photo 7). After a day's rest, Harry returned to Budowal to deal with the Sikhs there, but finding the fortress abandoned, he garrisoned the town and consolidated his forces with further reinforcements sent by Gough. He then advanced north to meet Ranjodh Singh.

The Sikhs had now been reinforced, amongst others, by the Avitabile Regiment, a highly professional infantry unit trained by the Italian mercenary, General Avitabile. With this addition, Ranjodh Singh was poised to take the offensive from his fortified position between the villages of Aliwal and Bhundri, with his back to the Sutlej River. Harry formed up with the cavalry in the rear and the infantry of two brigades, Wheeler's and Wilson's, in the front line, supported by two further brigades, Godby's and Hicks's, in the second, and continued his advance. At a range of 600 yards the Sikh artillery opened a devastating fire all along the line. Harry directed Godby and Hicks to move out from the second line, storm Aliwal on the right and then attack the Sikh defences in enfilade. These two brigades successfully took Aliwal and turned towards the Sikh centre, whereupon Ranjodh Singh brought up a body of cavalry to restore his collapsing flank.

At this point, Harry's cavalry brigade launched a series of charges against the Sikh horsemen, driving them back from Aliwal and leaving Godby free to advance beyond the Sikh line towards their camp on the bank of the Sutlej. Here the fords gave Ranjodh Singh's army the only escape route across the river. Under the pressure of this attack the Sikh line swung back along the river bank, turning on the village of Bhundri. When a force of Sikh cavalry emerged into the plain beyond Bhundri to threaten the British and Bengali flank, a squadron of the 16th Lancers and the 3rd Bengal Light Cavalry were ordered to drive this force back. The Lancers charged the Sikh horsemen with great energy and pursued them to the bank of the Sutlej. Returning from their charge, the squadron encountered the Avatabile Regiment of infantry, which formed up to receive a cavalry attack in a triangle, rather than a square; they adopted this formation so that if their line was penetrated, they could turn inward and bring fire to bear even amongst their own troops. Again the squadron charged home, in spite of receiving a devastating volley, and broke up the Sikh infantry. Two horse artillery guns, acting in support of the Lancers, unlimbered and opened fire on the remains of the Sikh regiment, completing the destruction. Eventually, the whole Regiment of the 16th Lancers delivered a last devastating charge, capturing the village of Bhundri and driving the garrison to the riverbank, thus concluding a great victory. On the anniversary of the Battle of Aliwal, the Queen's Royal Lancers, the descendants of the 16th Lancers, crimp the pennons on their lances in crimson to commemorate the dried blood sticking to them after the battle. The 53rd of Foot (later the King's Shropshire Light Infantry) followed up behind the cavalry and cleared Bhundri of the remaining determined pockets of Sikhs.

While the cavalry were engaged on the flanks, the British and Bengali infantry regiments, supported by artillery, pressed on over the Sikh defences, forcing them back to the Sutlej. As the Sikhs waded through the fords to escape across the river, a battery of Sikh gunners unhitched their guns and brought them into action on the river bank to cover the

# THE BATTLE OF ALIWAL

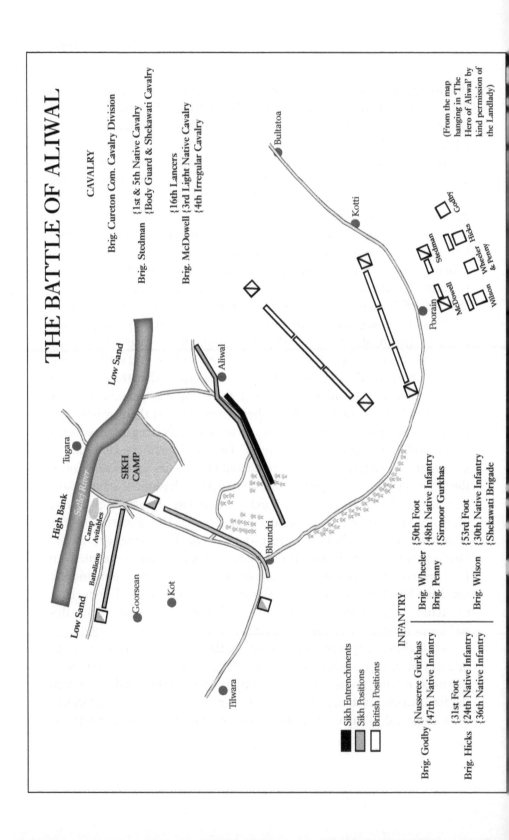

CAVALRY

Brig. Cureton Com. Cavalry Division

Brig. Stedman {1st & 5th Native Cavalry
{Body Guard & Shekawati Cavalry

{16th Lancers
Brig. McDowell {3rd Light Native Cavalry
{4th Irregular Cavalry

(From the map hanging in 'The Hero of Aliwal' by kind permission of the Landlady)

INFANTRY

Brig. Godby {Nusseree Gurkhas
{47th Native Infantry

{31st Foot
Brig. Hicks {24th Native Infantry
{36th Native Infantry

Brig. Wheeler {50th Foot
Brig. Penny {48th Native Infantry
{Sirmoor Gurkhas

{53rd Foot
Brig. Wilson {30th Native Infantry
{Shekawati Brigade

Sikh Entrenchments
Sikh Positions
British Positions

retreat, but they fired only one salvo before being overrun by the pursuing British troops. Ranjodh Singh attempted to bring some of his guns back across the river, but only two reached the far bank, two more being abandoned in the water and a further two sank irretrievably in quicksand.

The gunfire could be heard at Sobraon, some 50 miles away, and Gough realized that it signified Harry's triumph. The success at Aliwal was important for a number of reasons. Few battles are ever fought without mistakes being made, but this was one of them. Not only did it make Harry's reputation as a general in the eyes of the troops he led, but it gave those troops an overwhelming degree of self-confidence. They had faced the best the Sikhs could produce and had beaten them. The Bengali soldiers in particular, who were rightly terrified of the Sikhs, now knew that the latter were not the Gods of War they professed to be. Cooperation and coordination between the cavalry, artillery and infantry worked effectively, unlike previous engagements which had been so heavily criticized by Harry. India now knew that the danger of invasion by the warlike and bloodthirsty Sikhs had been swept away, people restored their loyalty to the Crown and those in the cantonments could breathe again. In England, the news of the great victory at Aliwal caused widespread rejoicing, and accolades were heaped on Harry and his men. Awards for gallantry had not, of course, been created by then, although officers were presented with medals for distinguished service – the gold medals in the Peninsula for example. The Peninsula medal, for all ranks, was not awarded until 1847 (see plate section, photo 8). However, recognition for valuable service could be given by promotion to brevet rank and inclusion in orders of chivalry, notably the Order of the Bath, of which Harry was a Companion, a Knight and a holder of the Knight Grand Cross! After Aliwal, fourteen officers were made Companions of the Bath and thirty-two were promoted to brevet rank (see plate section, photo 12). Rank and file had to be content with their 'General Service' medals. Pubs were called the 'Hero of Aliwal', and one exists today in Whittlesey, although it is a rather pale successor to its original (see plate section, photo 24). Harry marched his triumphant troops back to rejoin Gough's main army on 7 February, where they were received with great celebration. Harry wrote a dispatch, in his own, barely decipherable, handwriting, which exists today (see plate section, photo 11). But there was one battle still to fight: Sobraon.

The Sikh position at Sobraon consisted of a well-fortified, crescent-shaped bridgehead on the south side of the Sutlej, covered by guns on the higher north bank of the river. A reserve of mainly cavalry also remained on the far side. Gough was determined to close with the enemy in his usual robust way before the rainy and disease-laden season arrived. The Commander-in-Chief gave out his orders to his divisional commanders on 9 February for a full-blown, frontal, daylight attack, to be preceded by a heavy bombardment. Gough rejected Hardinge's suggestion of a diversionary force crossing the river further up, by night, to attack the Sikhs in the rear flank, for fear this would significantly weaken his forces. Harry had severe misgivings about Gough's plan. In his view, it completely failed to concentrate a maximum amount of force at a given point of weakness in the enemy's defence. Instead, the whole army was evenly spread out. Nevertheless, he did what he was told and deployed his now depleted Division onto the right flank.

Gough decided to initiate the attack on the south-east of the Sikhs' position with General Dick's Division, while Gilbert's Division and Harry's kept the enemy occupied. Troops set off at 3.00am to be in position by first light and take advantage of the preliminary barrage. A thick mist, which did not evaporate until 6.00am prevented any action until then, at which point the guns opened up. There was then a disaster. The heavy batteries, short of gunners, had to borrow soldiers from the field batteries, many of whom had no experience of operating the larger guns. Due to the recent arrival of the siege train and the lack of time for preparation, insufficient ammunition had been brought up to the gun positions, which were too far back. By about 8.30am the gun ammunition had run out, with little damage inflicted on the Sikh positions, so it was not until about 9.00am, that Dick's Division started their assault. The Sikhs held them well and Gough directed Gilbert and Harry to put in feint attacks to relieve the pressure on Dick, but to little effect. So much so that Gough then had no alternative but to order full-scale assaults. Harry's division engaged in fierce and bloody hand-to-hand fighting which reminded him of Badajoz and Waterloo. For the whole Division, the outcome was in the balance during prolonged fierce fighting. Even his usual optimism was dented, but eventually his own and the other two divisions advanced steadily, pushing the Sikhs back to the river. During the night heavy rain had swollen the river level by 7 feet, all the fords were submerged and all the pontoon bridges were swept away. Many of the enemy drowned and others were killed by Gough's, now effective, gunnery. The Sikhs lost about 9,000 men and all sixty-seven of their guns; the British lost 2,280 men including General Dick, who had lost an arm in the Peninsula, and two brigade commanders. Harry lost a higher percentage of his Division than at Aliwal, and nearly all his staff had been wounded, some more than once. Many had horses shot under them. Harry himself, with his charmed life as ever, was unscathed, but his ADC, Edward Hildich, was badly wounded in the arm and shoulder. He was evacuated to Ferozepore, which prevented Harry from going to visit him.

Soldiers helped themselves to a considerable amount of booty from the Sikh camp and, indeed, Harry received a large slice of prize money, enabling him to pay off debts and briefly reinstate his finances. Ever thoughtful of the worry he continued to cause Juana, who was recovering from a tropical fever in Simla, Harry now had time to write her a loving letter, full of all their secret code words. Harry himself remained immensely popular with his soldiers – he talked their language, swore like they did and instinctively knew what worried or upset them. He led from the front and, while tough on them, he was equally tough on himself. He looked after them as well as conditions allowed and reduced risk as far as possible. Particular favourites of his were the 50th of Foot, who were known as the 'Dirty Half Hundred', which of course they loved. Sobraon ended the war – for the moment – against the Sikhs. The Khalsa, the tough and highly disciplined army, and a major factor in the Sikh ruling dynasty, was effectively destroyed and the rulers in Lahore eagerly negotiated a peace.

Harry and Juana were soon reunited in Simla and happily read together the numerous letters of congratulation that flooded in, including one from Harry's beloved Duke. Harry, characteristically, brushed aside the loss of baggage at Budowal and the perception that he had failed to attack the Sikhs there. He turned it to his advantage, saying that, had he done so, Ranjodh Singh would have been less bold and less likely, therefore, to have faced Harry at Aliwal. A baronetcy was conferred on Harry and, unusually, 'of Aliwal' was to go after his name. 'Supporters' for his coat of arms would be a rifleman from the Rifle Brigade and another from the 52nd of Foot (later the Oxfordshire and Buckinghamshire Light Infantry – indeed, even later, with the Rifle Brigade, 60th and 43rd, to become the famous Greenjackets). Sadly the baronetcy, unlike the viscountcies and baronies to Hardinge and Gough, carried no pension. Nevertheless, Harry had been raised to Knight Grand Cross of the Order of the Bath (GCB) and promoted substantive Major General. The latter, however, meant he was now appointed District Commander in Cawnpore. This was not an enviable posting, situated as it was in land that was either excruciatingly hot or pouring with rain. Juana, against Harry's protests, as ever, determined to join him, even though it meant a 500-mile journey. Harry's health by now, after non-stop action, was deteriorating and he needed Juana's love and companionship. Additionally, they both longed for home and, with some clever arrangements by the Headquarters staff, they left India on sick leave, arriving in England on 29 April 1847 after an absence of eighteen years.

Harry and Juana had enjoyed the well-earned praise they had received in India after the Battle of Aliwal, but this was nothing to their enthusiastic welcome when their ship docked at Southampton. The General Officer Commanding the area made the formal welcome in front of cheering crowds – to be followed by the civic leaders of Southampton. Harry replied to the address of welcome at the civic banquet by saying that if he had rendered good service to his country it was to the fine soldiers he commanded that he was indebted. He is rarely mentioned in history books, but for the summer of 1847 he was the national hero, and with Juana by his side they were feted wherever they went.

They had returned from Bombay in a steamer, and to their surprise and delight – in contrast to Harry's frantic rides with coach and horses from Portsmouth years before – they travelled up to London in their own private train, pulled by a steam engine. When they arrived in London, they were inundated with invitations, notable among them from Queen Victoria, the Duke of Wellington, the Lord Mayor of London and Sir Robert Peel. One of their first engagements was to dine with the young Queen Victoria and Prince Albert. She recorded that Harry 'was a fine old man' who seemed pleased at her praises, said that he would always serve her and hoped that all her subjects would do so too. On 20 May, with Juana by his side, he received the Freedom of the City of London at the Guildhall. He replied, again paying tribute to the British soldier, and concluded that 'as long as England is true to herself and loyal to her sovereign she will stand as the paramount power in the world.' Perhaps even more moving for them was a dinner the same evening when they were guests of honour for the veterans of the Light Division, including John Colborne (Lord Seaton) whom Juana warmly embraced, Sir John Bell, Sir Andrew Barnard, Johnny Kincaid – still passionate about Juana – and Harry's brother Tom. The Times recorded this famous occasion in great detail, saying a hundred famous soldiers dined in London, and no capital could reproduce so memorable a reunion. On all sides, Sir Harry Smith received the congratulations of his countrymen, and for once the metropolitan season 'is supplied with a reasonable object of admiration'. It noted that Harry's coat of arms for his baronetcy was based on the achievements of his youth – Ciudad Rodrigo, the Pyrenees and the Rifles, and concluded that the previous rendezvous for this fine group of veterans of the Light Division would have been at Vitoria or the walls of Toulouse.

Harry's frenetic energy throughout his life ensured that the image of him is of a young man. An interesting comment, therefore, came from Lord Malmesbury who dined with Harry, now sixty, and Juana, aged forty-nine, on another May evening. He wrote: 'General Sir Harry Smith was the great lion of the evening. He is a little old man, very clever looking. She is a Spanish woman who has been very handsome.'

On 30 June 1847, Harry and Juana, as befitted the nation's celebrities, left London on another special steam train bound for Whittlesey, which stopped first at Ely. Their welcome there was described by Professor Sedgwick, the Master of Trinity, who had known Harry as a boy: 'The entry into Ely was triumphant. Thousands were assembled, with flags, branches of laurel and joyful anxious faces.' The Dean of Ely lent Sedgwick a horse so that he could join the triumphal procession led by a mounted trumpeter, together with the Chief Constable, the band with drums and fifes of the Scots Fusilier Guards, then Harry mounted on his favourite horse, Aliwal, and Juana riding in a coach. The Dean, the Reverend Peacock, presided at a magnificent lunch. He spoke of Harry as a valiant leader in the field, and as someone 'who was able to conciliate a foe and turn the enemies of the British Empire into its friends'.

After the celebrations in Ely, Harry and Juana and many other notables travelled the 20 miles to Whittlesey, where they faced another enthusiastic welcome. Professor Sedgwick again described the occasion. 'The procession moved through the town, with a guard of honour of the Whittlesey Yeomanry, commanded by Harry's brother, Captain Charles Smith, who had also fought at Waterloo.' Sedgwick noted that when they passed the old family home, Harry was deeply affected and 'the tears rolled down his weather beaten but fine face'. He and Juana attended a ball that evening and the next day were honoured by a formal dinner. Lord Hardwicke proposed the toast to Lady Smith and Harry replied, using the occasion to confirm his continuing love for Juana. He said he would have been less than a man if he had not sought the hand of the helpless but heroic girl at the siege of Badajoz. She had followed him, often in sanguinary circumstances, to every quarter of the globe with a devotion he found difficult to describe. She had watched him on the field of battle and had tended him in moments of pain and suffering. On the rare occasions when they were parted, he always felt her presence as his guardian angel. Finally, he thanked them again for their tributes to Juana and he knew she deserved them all. They stayed for a few days in Whittlesey with his brother Charles, Harry responding emotionally to the tributes of 'his playmates, schoolmates and townsmen'. Then, with Juana, he travelled to other fenland towns and villages, including Wisbech, where he opened a museum.

Their reception in Ely and Whittlesey had been moving occasions, but the climax was still to come. In early July, Harry was again the celebrity guest at a major function in Cambridge. He was due to receive an honorary degree from Cambridge University, but Sedgwick, knowing that Queen Victoria, Prince Albert and the Duke of Wellington would be present, invited Harry to come early and stay in Trinity College, where he was Master. On Monday, 5 July, Harry received his degree, and there was a luncheon for sixty people, including the Queen and Prince Albert. Later Sedgwick hosted a dinner in Trinity for 300, 'and we had more numbers and more fun'. There were cheers for the Duke when he left the Senate House, but he calmed the cheering and, putting his arm around Harry's shoulder, called, 'This is the man you should cheer, he is the hero of the day.' Harry burst into tears and said, 'I little thought I should live to hear such kind words from my old chief.' Harry's admiration for the Duke is well known, but this incident illustrates the Duke's affection for Harry. Sedgwick added, 'Indeed, he is more like the Duke's son.'

Throughout the summer Harry and Juana received gifts and addresses wherever they went. In Glasgow, their kindness during the difficult post-war times had not been forgotten and they were sent a magnificent piece of silver, together with an invitation for Harry to become their Member of Parliament. He was flattered by this offer, but once again was faced with a financial dilemma – at that time MPs were not paid and he still lacked an assured income. But would Governorship of the Cape put this right?

# Chapter 8

## Governor at the Cape
## September 1847 to February 1850

Although Harry and Juana had revelled in the euphoria of their welcome back to England, in mixing with the top brass and the aristocracy, and even in dining with Queen Victoria and Prince Albert, despite his brilliant military success, Harry had not benefited financially from his Indian campaigns as much as he might have expected. It is true that he had been rewarded with a baronetcy and Aliwal was proudly displayed on his coat of arms, together with an elephant, but he had not been financially rewarded in the way Gough had been for the Sikh campaign, or Napier, who was far junior to Harry, had been for taking over Sind. As ever Harry and Juana had been spendthrift and had continued their fairly light-hearted approach to money matters.

It was therefore a great relief to them both when, during a conversation Harry had with the Duke, that Wellington mentioned, almost as an aside, that he would be going to the Cape as Governor and would be promoted to Lieutenant General. In an age of heroes, a combination of circumstance had suddenly favoured Harry. The current Governor, Pottinger, had been totally inadequate and his inept handling of a new Kaffir war on the frontier had been carried out at a very substantial cost in both lives and money. Suddenly, Harry seemed the obvious choice to replace him – his military successes were still fresh in the minds of the Government, and they remembered, too, his vigorous execution of the frontier policy of D'Urban, which had now been vindicated. Pottinger had appeared to stumble from one disaster to another and merely asked for more and more troops, while Harry, who had kept up his interest in South African affairs, had recently sent Wellington a detailed memorandum about the frontier situation. He was absolutely delighted at his appointment, and wrote to his old friend and colleague D'Urban to say that he would go and 're-do what Lord Glenelg so ably did undo'. To his further delight, before they left for Cape Town, Harry had several conferences with the Duke himself on both the strategy and tactics of the frontier question, and also on supplies and logistics.

For Juana it had been the happiest summer since landing at Portsmouth in April 1847 on their return from India. Now, packing up to go to Cape Town was very different, with no great rush and only a few days to catch a waiting ship. As the Governor's lady she could indulge her joy in fashion, helped by her numerous nieces, all so fond of their generous and attractive aunt. With their financial situation assured, Juana could purchase a wardrobe suitable for her new grand position. No longer the slim young bride of Badajoz, she was now fifty years old and a comely matron with a host of good friends and relations. Harry and Juana, still excited by the challenge, made a leisurely journey from London, reaching Portsmouth in mid-September. Here they spent another ten enjoyable days, being fêted with balls and dinners with old army friends. A highlight for them both came when, at a dinner with the Rifles, Harry proudly replied to the toast of 'Lady Smith'. The next day, 24 September 1847, they embarked on the ship *Vernon* bound for Cape Town.

During their relaxed and trouble-free voyage, Harry turned his mind to the problems he was likely to face when he arrived. He still felt bitter about his dismissal in 1837 and the role in that distressing episode of the evangelical missionary lobby. He was therefore reassured to discover that the Church of England was looking positively towards Cape Colony, had appointed a Bishop of Cape Town and was actively recruiting chaplains to work in the diocese. Lord Glenelg, the former Colonial Secretary, had recalled D'Urban, the Governor, and had appointed in his place Sir George Napier. The immediate consequence was the emigration from the Colony of numbers of Dutch farmers (described by D'Urban as 'a brave, patient, industrious, orderly, and religious people'). The policy entrusted to the new Governor was that of entering into alliances with the Kaffir chiefs, but experience soon taught him that this was futile and the only possible course was that which had been pursued by his predecessor and Harry. 'My own experience and what I saw with my own eyes,' he declared to a Parliamentary Committee in 1851, 'have confirmed me that I was wrong and Sir Benjamin D'Urban perfectly right; that if he meant to keep Kaffirland under British rule, the only way of doing so was by having a line of forts and maintaining troops in them'.

In the years between the Smiths leaving Cape Town in 1837 and their return in 1847, more and more Boer farmers had trekked north with their families and cattle into the open areas around the Orange and Vaal rivers. During the early 1840s, Britain, conscious of the growing population on the East Coast, had also taken over the very large area called Natal, and in a belated tribute to Harry's old friend, named the capital Durban. In all his dealings with the different peoples on the frontier, Harry's conviction and policy never wavered: that he was bringing the blessings and benefits of Christianity and civilization to the whole area and to all the tribes in it. In all humility, he hoped that he had previously sown some seeds, which might now bear fruit.

The *Vernon* arrived in Cape Town on 1 December 1847 with a tumultuous welcome for the Governor and his Lady. They instantly felt that they were back among old friends, even though the Peninsula veterans were thinning out. Almost at once news came of more trouble on the frontier and Harry reassured the rather apprehensive people by merely remarking, 'Doing something they ought not, I'll be bound.' A measure of their worry is shown by the vast crowds who turned out to welcome Harry and Juana with festivities lasting through the night. After all, here was the man who had brought peace and prosperity to the whole border area and whose vigorous actions had subsequently been vindicated. Since then his brisk and confident policies had been proved in the harsh terrain of the Punjab and in the Sikh wars. Surely he could not possibly go wrong in dealing with a few restless Kaffirs on the frontier? Confirming the warmth and sincerity of the welcome at the formal banquet, the Chief Justice, dropping all formality addressed them as 'Harry Smith and his wife'.

Sadly, a situation which appeared to have everything in its favour was to prove fraught with grave and unexpected difficulties. Harry's impetuous and youthful vigour, which had won him so many victories and successes, now developed into an explosive arrogance and an autocratic attitude which speedily offended many of those who had welcomed him back. His former quick temper became more furious, and his blood-curdling threats and colourful language created an atmosphere in which few dared to express a contrary opinion. It seemed that he was at his best when his exuberance was curbed by a more senior figure – like Gough or D'Urban – but when that rein was removed he was dangerously impetuous.

Taking just a few days to grasp the situation in the Cape, Harry set off on 11 December – not this time on horseback – but by ship to go to Port Elizabeth to tackle the problems of the Kaffirs across the whole frontier area. The upheavals on the frontier had been stirred up by one incident and then the bungled attempts by Pottinger to overcome the ensuing uprisings among the Xhosa people. Two of the most powerful chiefs, Macomo and Sandile had eventually been captured and were held in Grahamstown. When Harry arrived at Port Elizabeth and travelled on to Grahamstown, he was greeted at every stage with joyful welcomes. The people of the frontier had suffered severely from muddled policies incompetently enacted, and remembering Harry's previous success, they saw him as the new Governor who would solve all their problems.

Therefore, as soon as possible he had Chief Macomo brought before him. Macomo, an important and influential chief who had been restrained during the recent uprisings, advanced towards Harry and held out his hand. To the amazement of the large crowd who had been assembled for this occasion, Harry forced Macomo to lie on the floor, placed his foot on the chief's neck and shouted that in future this was how all enemies would be treated. This public humiliation created a bitter and life-long enemy of Macomo and seemed totally at odds with the cordial relations Harry had enjoyed with all the chiefs in his previous campaigns on the frontier.

His initial blunder with the humiliation of Macomo was followed by a second in Grahamstown, where he had been greeted by triumphal arches reading 'Do justice and Fear Not'. As part of the welcoming ceremony, Harry announced that the Kaffirs would be prostrated under his feet. Another Xhosa chief, Sandile, who had been more fully involved in the recent troubles, but who was young and immature compared to Macomo, was brought forward. Again Harry refused to shake his hand, announcing that he would be punished for his folly and treachery, and would kiss the Governor's foot as a token of submission. Harry had been advised not to release Sandile, but he ignored the advice, and sent Sandile away hoping, wrongly, that he would go and spread the message that the Governor must be obeyed. These two incidents caused deep concern to many who had welcomed Harry on his return, but now questioned the wisdom of the new policy.

Harry's critics maintained that his head had been turned by all the adulation he had received in England after the victory of Aliwal, and that his overbearing arrogance now caused a succession of disasters. He had set out on this latest journey convinced that he could bring the unrest on the frontier to a swift conclusion.

Harry continued his rapid tour of the colony, announcing the extension of British territory to the Keiskama River. This area was to be called Victoria and would be extended north towards the Orange River. Proposed settlements in this area included Alice – after his sister Mrs Sargant – Whittlesey, Ely and even Juanasburg, suggesting perhaps that his new position had indeed gone to his head. As his progress continued, the local people and settlers alike gave him an enthusiastic reception. He reached King William's Town on 23 December 1847 and called a great meeting of chiefs and people. In a theatrical performance, having ensured that all weapons had been removed from the braves, with the band playing 'See the conquering hero comes', he entered the assembly on horseback and in full-dress uniform, wearing all his decorations and surrounded by his staff. In a lengthy address, he informed the gathering that they were once again under British rule, with laws which would emphasize Christianity and civilization. Then, using a device which had succeeded ten years before, he held out a lance – the symbol of war – and a brass knob as the symbol of the rule of law. While he remained on his horse, each chief had to come forward, kiss his foot and touch either the lance or the brass knob. They, wisely, chose the brass knob. Such formal occasions were repeated in many places.

On 7 January 1848, he held a great meeting of the chiefs and all the important local people, including missionaries. Here he elaborated his policy, demanding that they gave up abhorrent practices like murder, rape, witchcraft and the buying of wives. Then, fomenting his fury, he swore that if they disobeyed him, 'I will eat you up', and with further threats, he warned them that if they dared to make war he would destroy them. Finally, in a famous – or infamous – incident, repeating a trick he had played years before, he indicated a wagon on a nearby crest which his engineers had filled with explosive. He shouted, 'I am so powerful that I only have to point to that wagon and it will blow up.' After it blew up, he added, 'That is what will happen to you if you do not behave yourselves.'

These histrionics during his tour of the frontier were backed up by a positive and vigorous policy to help keep the peace. Army units were used to enforce law and order, but were clearly instructed that force should only be used as a last resort. The London government had demanded retrenchment, and they supported a policy of encouraging soldiers to retire and take up generous offers of land in military villages along the frontier. This brought more British settlers to the frontier area and it saved the cost of repatriating time-expired men, but it did not always succeed. Many old soldiers turned to drink and caused trouble with Hottentot women. Harry also had to overcome his understandable distrust of the missionaries and he started to encourage their activities on the frontier with grants of land, the development of roads, the establishment of schools and farms, and the fostering of trade.

Fairly soon, Harry had to come to grips with other long-term issues and problems which would affect the future of the colony, and indeed the whole of southern Africa. To encourage the development of the eastern region, a new port, to be called East London, was established at the mouth of the Buffalo River below King William's Town. He had hoped to bring some order into the turbulent territories in the areas of the Vaal and Orange Rivers, but his more aggressive policies hardly achieved this. He had already offended Macomo, the Chief of the Xhosa, and when he met Adam Kok, a Griqua chief, he threatened to hang him if he did not sign an agreement. More significant for the

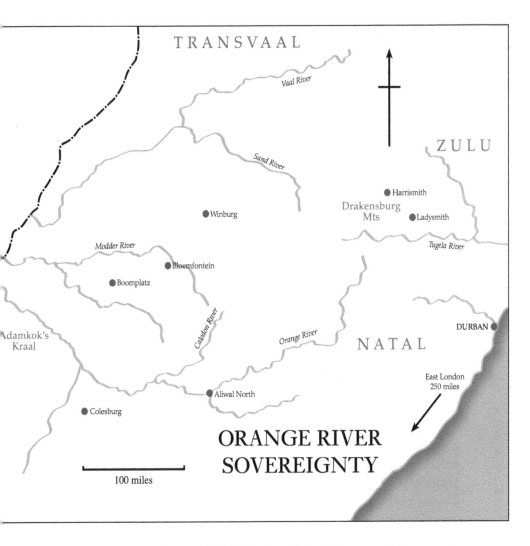

future were his meetings with Moshesh, chief of the proud Basutos in their mountain kingdom, and Dingaan the Zulu leader, a descendant of Shaka. Both of these chiefs had already clashed with the Boer settlers who added an explosive element into the situation. Harry was already backing the idea of the Orange River Sovereignty when he met Pretorius, the intrepid Voortrekker leader, who warned him that if the Sovereignty was imposed he would lead his people further north out of the clutches of the British. He then left to consult the various Boer commando leaders. There is little doubt that Harry seriously deluded himself about his influence over the Boers in the frontier areas. Because they had initially welcomed him back with great enthusiasm, he found it difficult to believe that they would not accept his policies.

Without waiting for a reply from Pretorius, Harry proclaimed the Orange River Sovereignty, which brought 50,000 square miles of land under British control, including huge potential problems with resentful Voortrekkers, Moshesh and the Basuto, the Zulus and the Xhosa. With a wildly optimistic attitude, he left the security of this vast and volatile region to a major and sixty Cape Mounted Rifles. He argued, 'The Boers are my children.' In addition to the problems on the ground, Harry had to gain the agreement of Whitehall, which in general was opposed to any extension of the frontier. He argued consistently that if an area was taken over and civilized, it would eventually bring in substantial revenue. London was not entirely convinced, but Grey, the Colonial Secretary, felt that they could not once again withdraw from a territory which had just been taken over. However, very stern advice was issued 'in terms as explicit as any that can be employed, and under sanctions as grave as can be devised, that the acquisition of any further territory is banned'. The opposition in London warned that they were being committed to an endless succession of expensive frontier wars.

In spite of all these problems which Harry had tried to tackle during his weeks on the frontier, he was again given a wildly enthusiastic welcome when he returned to Cape Town. He was still seen as the brilliant High Commissioner, who in a few weeks had sorted out the frontier problems, which under previous inept leadership had bedevilled the colony for years.

Harry had only been back home for a very short time when he received a message from Major Warden, who had been left in charge on the frontier, asking for troop reinforcements because Pretorius was encouraging revolt. Harry then sent a very odd manifesto, which was a mixture of dire threats, appeals to the Boers as fellow Christians, bloodcurdling threats backed by Old Testament quotations and a final prayer for peace. Pretorius hesitated about his next step, partly because his wife was terminally ill, but there was very strong feeling among the

Boer trekkers and on 12 July 1849, they persuaded Pretorius to advance to Winburg, challenging the British presence. When the Boers approached, the British magistrate rode off to Bloemfontein to warn Warden and the Cape Mounted Rifles, but, faced by a Boer commando, Warden could do little and he meekly surrendered. Pretorius put him and his supporters in wagons and sent them south.

Harry was not likely to acquiesce in such a situation, immediately ordering troops to advance to Colesburg and offering £1,000 reward for the capture of Pretorius. He sent a hurried dispatch to London, assuring Grey that he would rapidly settle the issue and would make the rebel Boers pay for everything. With Grey announcing this in the Commons and the opposition furiously attacking yet another expensive frontier war, Harry rushed off to take command, leaving Juana once again to worry about the danger threatening her Enrique. Units available to him included some Highlanders and a few companies of the Rifles, which Harry dispersed along the frontier. He then set off on another frantic ride, with his ADC Holdich (later General Sir Edward Holdich), and arrived in Colesburg on 9 August.

Pretorius and his commando were drawn up on a river bank near Colesburg, protected by trenches, and after Harry's arrival Pretorius sent a petition asking him to withdraw. Harry faced a complex situation with elements which would bedevil South African history for decades to come. Some of the local chiefs offered to support him, but he refused to use native forces against the Boers. At the same time, the Boers themselves were divided and as they did in the Boer War of 1899-1902, resented central discipline, and often went off from the commando to look after their farms and families.

Pretorius held a strongly fortified post on the far bank of the Orange River, but on 22 August, when Harry's forces started to cross, the Boers withdrew to another position. This was a foolish move because the river was in full spate and an opposed crossing could have wrought havoc on the attackers. A subaltern from 45th Regiment wrote home with a vivid description of Harry: 'He is the most extraordinary man I ever met, he is all energy and works from daylight to dark. Swears most awfully at everyone from his ADC down to the drummer boy.' His forces, which included the Cape Mounted Rifles, units from the Argyll and

Sutherland Highlanders and the Rifle Brigade, and some Boers who had accepted the Manifesto, took several days to cross the river. (On 29 March, Harry had issued a Manifesto of a typically unconventional kind. He encouraged the farmers to remember all the benefits he had lately conferred on them, such as freedom from nominal subjection to native chiefs, and to contrast the misery from which he had tried to release them, with the happiness of their friends and cousins living under the Colonial Government. If they 'compelled him to wield the fatal sword, after all he had attempted to do for them, the crime be on their own heads'. He concluded with a prayer to the Almighty in which he suggested that the farmers might unite with him.) Finally, and even more surprisingly, a group of Griquas under Adam Kok, whom Harry had recently berated, joined him. Perhaps they objected to the Boers more than the British.

After crossing the river, the British force advanced across flat country until they came to a range of hills where, as expected, Pretorius took a stand near a farm called Boomplatz. This hardly deserves to be called a battle, for Pretorius, although he chose the ground carefully to ambush the British, only had about 500 men, and half of those were left to guard the wagons. He planned that, as the British approached the farmhouse, he would attack them from three sides. The British advanced in a leisurely way, with Harry still hoping that a compromise might be reached. He sent a unit ahead with orders not to fire, for he could not believe that his friends the Boers would ever fire at him. But he was grievously mistaken – as the leading units approached the farm, the Boers opened fire from three sides. Several men were hit and Harry himself was wounded. With a stream of curses he turned round and led the attack. To the surprise of the Boers, Harry had several 6- and 9-pounder guns in reserve, which he rapidly brought into play and peppered the Boer position with grapeshot. The disciplined and well-trained regulars made a strong attack on the Boer's left flank and although there was a spirited resistance from the farmhouse, which wounded the colonel of the Rifles, the Boers rapidly retreated. They complained bitterly that Harry had used Griquas and Hottentots against them, but he rejected their complaints and rewarded the Hottentots with extra biscuits and tobacco.

This brief clash cost the British about fifty killed and wounded, with the Boer casualties nearer 200, though all these figures have been hotly disputed. Historians of nineteenth-century wars know that an occasional nought creeps into the numbers of battle casualties to enhance a victory or excuse a defeat. Harry's wound was duly reported and Queen Victoria, who had personally awarded Juana a special medal for her brave performance on the elephants at Ferozepore, now awarded her a pension of £500 a year at the thought that she might have been left a widow.

During September, Harry set about restoring law and order in Bloemfontein and setting up a new administration. Two rebels were executed but another Boer was pardoned and given a civilian post. The disciplined action of the Argyll and Sutherland Highlanders had made a great impact, and in the aftermath of the fighting Harry's mixture of fierceness and kindness seems to have worked – at least temporarily. He left small garrisons of infantry companies and an artillery unit with the 9-pounder guns which had been so effective at Boomplatz. Durbars and formal parades were held in different places in order to bolster the regime. Harry was particularly pleased that Moshesh, the distinguished chief of the Basuto people, appeared to have become a firm ally. In emphasizing Christianity and civilization, he insisted on frequent church services, with confident appeals to Almighty God. Ever punctilious for things to be done with dignity, on one occasion he was reading the lesson when a dog intruded. He had reached the words 'And the Lord said', when he broke off and added, 'Take that bloody dog out of here.'

After several hectic weeks on the border, Harry set off back to Cape Town. At every stage he was greeted by large and enthusiastic crowds, and then at Port Elizabeth he embarked on the steamer *Phoenix* and sailed home arriving on 21 October.

Among the thousands of people who turned out to greet Harry on his return to Cape Town in October 1848, none was more relieved than Juana, who from the time of Badajoz onwards had dreaded the separation when Harry was called away on duty, and lived in a state of tense anxiety when he was in action during a war. Her anxiety turned to anguish when she heard that he had been wounded and it was little comfort that she shared her concern with Queen Victoria. She was overjoyed when Harry returned, but alarmed about his haggard looks and exhausted appearance. Now at last she felt they could really enjoy their role as the popular and respected Governor and his Lady in a society which was rapidly developing, because so many of the new steamships called at the Cape on the way to India. While he was away, she had lacked the confidence, and also the energy, to play a really decisive role herself, and in a gossipy expatriate community there had been the beginnings of some grumbling criticism. With her patrician Spanish background, a certain haughtiness seems to have appeared in her demeanor, and her fondness for Spanish fashions and for colourful Indian silks and fabrics was not popular with a basically farming and frontier community. One of her attempts to help the different communities sadly backfired. She tried to foster links with the Indian and Malay communities in the Cape, and occasionally attended displays of nautch dancing – a sensuous dance by women for the erotic entertainment of men, and even then considered dubious. This was seized on by the largely puritanical Boer residents and caused some concern to Bishop Gray in the newly established Anglican diocese. He stoutly defended Juana but was more worried about Harry who, although a staunch Anglican, whose correspondence and speeches frequently referred to Almighty God, seemed to have a remarkable tolerance of other faiths, and even considered opening Islamic schools.

Although Harry's over-optimistic hopes for peace on the frontier between the Bantu and the Boers initially seemed justified, he and Juana were soon to be caught up in another totally different and controversial issue, the focus of which was in Cape Town. For many years the new colonies in Australia had been used for the transportation of convicts, and the system was well established in what appeared to be a vast and empty area, with very few native peoples. Britain had a totally inadequate number of prisons and the situation had been seriously exacerbated by the results of the Irish famine of the mid-1840s. This put huge pressure on Whitehall and in November 1848 – a couple of weeks after he returned from the frontier – Harry received a dispatch from Earl Grey, the Colonial Secretary, asking if Cape Colony would be prepared to receive what were called 'ticket of leave' convicts, i.e. men who had served their time and were considered reliable. Grey supported the idea on the grounds that a useful supply of labour would be provided to help with the economic development of the Colony. He added that the majority of the convicts would not be serious criminals or common felons, but either Irish political prisoners or those affected by the suffering of the Irish famine, whose crime might be stealing food to feed a starving family. It would be reasonable to employ them on public works. He concluded by stating that the British Government was facing a serious crisis and might have to pass an Order in Council designating Cape Colony as a place to which convicts could be sent. He wanted Harry to have due warning of this possibility and to have time to make the necessary arrangements.

For all his previous achievements and successes, this was a totally new and different problem for Harry to face, and it put him in a serious quandary. There was a very strong feeling among the settlers in Cape Town against the idea of admitting Britain's convicts, because of the perceived danger of criminal activity spreading to the native people. The personal feelings of Harry and of Juana, who had had longer to assess and understand local opinion, were entirely with the Cape people. Harry, whose whole professional military career had been based on discipline and obedience, and who, as a military commander, was accustomed to making serious and sometimes unpopular decisions, was to find himself increasingly torn between what appeared best in the Cape and what, as Governor, he had to carry out on the orders of Whitehall.

In his dispatch, Grey had used emollient phrases like 'a few hundred', and 'the idea is being considered', and Harry followed suit. He first mentioned the issue as 'a few Irish political offenders, not ordinary felons', and repeated that he was totally opposed to the idea of the Cape becoming a penal settlement. He stressed the duty of the Colony to help the Mother Country, just as the Mother Country had helped the Cape in its recent troubles. Such soft phrases instantly antagonized local leaders, who realized the wider threat. The merchant community immediately demanded full-scale consultation and public meetings, and related this issue to the current discussions about responsible government. Many dispatches and letters crossed between

Grey and Harry, and the situation was exacerbated by Grey's rather casual, aristocratic aloofness, by the instant and growing anger in the Cape, and by the slow communication between London and Cape Town.

Early in 1849 Harry and the colonists hoped that their protestations and massive petitions had been accepted, but a greater crisis was about to erupt because Grey had not been honest in his earlier dispatch to Harry. He had mentioned that an Order in Council was being considered, but he failed to say that in September 1848 it had already been passed, giving the British Government permission to send convicts to the Cape. The tone of Grey's dispatches rapidly grew harsher and he clearly expected Harry to force the issue through. Harry merely said he would do his best to carry out the Government's policy. While this increasingly tense correspondence continued, in February 1849, Grey sent a ship, the *Neptune*, with 300 convicts on board, to Bermuda. There the convicts would be landed and a similar number of 'ticket of leave' men would be taken on and delivered to Cape Town. It is clear that Grey expected Harry to enforce this decision.

When Harry returned home in October, Juana had been alarmed because he looked so haggard and exhausted, and for many weeks he failed to recover his normal vigour. As the weeks passed, she was reminded that early in the Peninsula campaign he had suffered severely from boils on his bottom, which had made it very difficult to ride a horse. In the spring of 1849, as a result of the pressure he was under, there was a recurrence of boils, and at the height of the convict crisis he was seriously ill with a large carbuncle on his neck. Juana had to call the doctor urgently and when he lanced the carbuncle Harry lost consciousness. For days he lay so seriously ill that no one was permitted to visit him and the Bishop organized prayers throughout the diocese. This was such a strain on Juana that she too needed medical treatment. The doctor considered that if Harry had not had a robust constitution he would have died.

As he slowly recovered, the fierce tension continued. Virtually all the colonists supported the Anti-Convict Association which had been formed to oppose British policy. Opposition was so strong that dozens of officials resigned, as did members of the Legislative Council. When it became known that the *Neptune* had left Bermuda and was heading for the Cape, the tension was racked up still further. The Anti-Convict Association and other bodies put forward more and more extreme threats and demands which put Harry in an almost impossible position. At heart he agreed with the colonists, but as Governor he had to carry out the policy dictated from Whitehall. In several letters during May and June 1849, he begged Grey to reconsider the decision because the opposition to the convicts was 'absolutely frantic'. He also reminded Grey that until the convict issue arose everything had been going very well.

The crisis came to a climax when the Order in Council was formally published in Cape Town on 15 June, and the whole community rose in opposition. The Anti-Convict Association threatened to ostracize anyone who had any contact whatsoever with the convicts when they arrived. Some businesses which had supported Harry were boycotted and financially ruined. The Association demanded that Harry ignore the Order in Council. On 18 June, in a reply charged with emotion, he stated: 'This is the anniversary of the Battle of Waterloo – for four and forty years I served my sovereign – I say it with pride – and I would rather that God Almighty strike me dead than disobey the orders of Her Majesty's Government, and thereby commit an act of open rebellion.' The pressure and tension on Harry and Juana became almost unbearable. Less than a year before they had been warmly greeted as old friends and as saviours of the Colony. Now they were reviled. The local paper mocked and derided them. The money subscribed for an equestrian statue for Harry was diverted to the Anti-Convict Association. On 20 June, the traditional Governor's Ball to celebrate the Queen's Accession took place. In the past people went to great lengths to obtain an invitation – now invitations were rudely returned. Many who had accepted now lacked the courage to face the wrath of their neighbours and stayed away. Once again the tension laid Harry low, but he rose from his sick bed to attend the Ball. The voice of the Governor, known for his rasping expletives and blood-curdling oaths, was too weak even to propose the loyal toast. There are several descriptions of the occasion. One said that his deathly pallor was accentuated by the drab green of his Rifles uniform which he proudly wore; another described how he looked as if he had risen from his coffin but was wearing full-dress uniform with all his decorations. Juana, though magnificently dressed in gold and black with an impressive array of diamonds, was noticeably agitated. Socially, the Ball was a complete disaster.

It became increasingly urgent that Harry made the necessary decisions to resolve the crisis. While he tended towards taking a strong line against the Association leaders, his advisers were afraid that such action in the highly volatile situation might provoke a rebellion which could be joined by the supporters of Pretorius on the frontier. The tension continued. The settlers realized that after one of the members of the Legislative Council died there was no longer a quorum to make legal decisions. No one could be found to take the vacant seat. On 10 July, the Court house, where Harry, using his prerogative as Governor, had introduced three new members, was surrounded by a howling mob. The local paper described with some relish how stones, filth and rotten eggs were thrown, and one of the new members was assaulted. Then Harry, leaning on the arm of his ADC Holdich, emerged from the building, and the crowd fell silent. He said, 'Gentlemen, I am glad to be amongst you. Believe me, my heart is with you.' This olive branch did not quell the disturbances, and under threats of further violence the three members resigned.

As the weeks passed, Harry attempted to bring home to Grey the gravity of the situation in both private letters and official dispatches. He wrote: 'The violence of the colonists upon the subject is inconceivable and it is widely felt that the Colony is on the brink of insurrection.' At the same time, the whereabouts of the *Neptune*, which had left Bermuda four months earlier, remained a mystery. Harry even wondered hopefully if Grey had diverted it elsewhere. One rumour suggested, even more hopefully, that it had sunk with all hands. Neither of these were true and on 19 September, the *Neptune*, which had been delayed in Brazil by sickness, arrived off Cape Town. Harry immediately ordered that it should anchor in Simon's Bay and should not communicate in any way with the shore. The actual arrival of the *Neptune* prompted immediate demands that it should be ordered to leave. The Anti-Convict Association made further impossible demands, but Harry made it clear that the *Neptune* would remain at anchor until further orders were received from London.

This decision bought some time, but it started another period of intense bitterness and violence. The Association demanded a complete boycott of the ship and of the government agencies supporting it. (The term 'boycott' was not actually coined until thirty years later, in similar circumstances in County Kerry, during the Irish Land Wars.) The boycott caused extensive disruption to trade and many businesses failed, while the army had to be used to provide bread, meat and milk for the ship, and to protect supplies brought from outside. Units were abused and attacked so that Harry had to exhort his troops to show forbearance and moderation, in spite of provocation. Farmers who brought in supplies were also attacked and their wagons overturned. The extremists even spread the rumour that there were many homosexuals among the convicts and if they were allowed in it would undermine the moral standards of the Colony. During October 1849, the extreme stance of the Association, which even punished children, gradually alienated the public, and supplying the *Neptune* became slightly easier. When Grey sent a dispatch announcing that he had abandoned the idea of establishing a permanent penal settlement, this reduced the tension, but it did not solve the problem of the *Neptune* and its unfortunate convicts anchored offshore for weeks.

While the situation in Cape Town slowly improved, the pressure on Harry continued because the colonists remained adamant that the convicts on the *Neptune* should not be landed, and Grey, despite all Harry's letters and dispatches, seemed not to accept the true position. The problems seemed endless for Harry and Juana while the fate of the convicts was unresolved. Grey continued to expect Harry to override the colonists and get the convicts ashore, and so in December 1849, Harry, in a moving and heart-rending message to Grey, wrote: 'God alone knows the devotion of my heart and soul to the Queen, Her Majesty's Government, and more especially to you, my Lord, under whom I accepted an Office tendered, but a point of honour cannot be conceded.'

Once again, slow communications made matters worse, and only in February 1850 was it learnt that Grey had finally given in and agreed that the convicts would go to Tasmania. It took even longer for him to write to Harry and apologize for taking a critical and unhelpful attitude during the crisis. He finally confirmed the Whitehall view that Harry had been correct in not admitting the convicts and hoped that their friendship had not been impaired. When Grey's decision became known in Cape Town there was widespread rejoicing and celebrations. In order to hasten its departure, supplies to revictual the *Neptune* were eagerly provided. Because the convicts had suffered such hardship while lying off Cape Town, they were offered a pardon when they reached Tasmania. Many of them rose to high office both in Australia and in America, including Sir Charles Duffy, who became Prime Minister of Victoria. The convict crisis finally passed, but it took a very heavy toll on Harry's health, and he never fully regained his old purposeful vigour. At the same time the bitter divisions among the people of the colony were never entirely healed.

# Chapter 9

# Anticlimax
# February 1850 to April 1852

W hile the convict crisis continued, it appeared that Harry's previous exertions had succeeded and the frontier was peaceful. In view of this, in 1850, in order to accede to Grey's demand for economy, Harry sent a battalion of the Rifles back to England. This left less than 2,000 troops to control the whole frontier and half of these were scattered about in different garrisons. The apparent peace masked some serious unrest. Several areas had suffered from plagues of locusts, and a severe drought had caused widespread suffering and loss of crops and cattle. Some chiefs were restless and resented Harry's high-handed attitude and his humiliation of Macomo. They realized that the Rifles had been sent home and they reckoned that the aggressive settler opposition to Harry over the convict issue had undermined his position. He was reassured when a number of chiefs offered to support him against the troublesome Gaikas, but once again he seriously overestimated his influence with the chiefs as he had done with the Boers. Much of the simmering resentment was brought to a head by a young religious fanatic, Mlanjeni, who claimed that his ancestors had told him to drive out the British. He also claimed that his potions could turn British bullets to water.

Harry, far from well and showing the heavy physical and psychological toll which the convict crisis had cost him, ignored Juana's desperate pleas and set off for the frontier, believing that he alone could quickly solve the problems. He sailed to Port Elizabeth, hurried on and

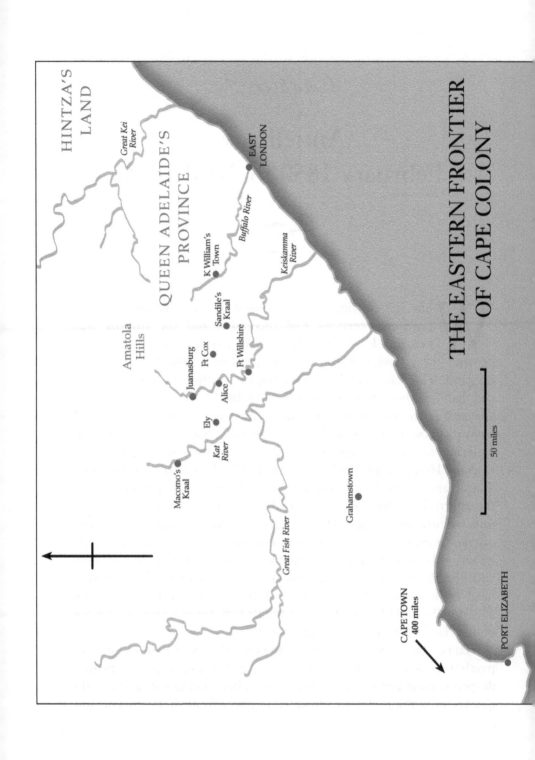

THE EASTERN FRONTIER
OF CAPE COLONY

HINTZA'S LAND

QUEEN ADELAIDE'S PROVINCE

Great Kei River

Buffalo River

EAST LONDON

K William's Town

Keiskamma River

Sandile's Kraal

Ft Cox

Ft Willshire

Amatola Hills

Juanasburg

Alice

Ely

Kat River

Macomo's Kraal

Great Fish River

Grahamstown

50 miles

CAPE TOWN
400 miles

PORT ELIZABETH

reached Fort Cox just before Christmas 1850 (see map on page 160). The Gaikas, including Macomo and Sandile, were now seriously aroused and were no longer overawed by Harry's threats. On Christmas Eve, when he heard of a gathering of warriors under Sandile, he sent a force of 600 men to deal with it. With little time for a reconnaissance, they had to advance through a narrow gorge beside a river. Sandile's men, showing admirable discipline, allowed them to move deep into the gorge and then attacked on three sides. The force managed to fight its way out, but at a cost of thirty lives. As the depleted force returned to Fort Cox, they passed the bodies of another detachment which had been massacred, the bodies left naked and grossly mutilated. At the same time, three of the military villages, which normally had good relations with the local tribes, were attacked, overwhelmed and most of the people murdered. Harry heard this news while he was beleaguered in Fort Cox and surrounded by thousands of Gaikas. To make matters worse, all the Kaffir police deserted and joined the rebels. Such was the power of the assembled warriors surrounding Fort Cox that two attempts by Colonel Somerset to raise the siege had been beaten off.

After the failure of the second attempt, Harry's position was extremely dangerous and precarious. What a prize his capture would be for Macomo and the Gaika chiefs! Already renowned for his epic rides, he now undertook the most dangerous of all. He selected 200 men of the Cape Mounted Rifles (CMR), disguised himself as one of them, complete with uniform, then, in the middle of the posse, broke through the besiegers and rode frantically for King William's Town 20 miles away. The group had to fight several fierce skirmishes on the way, but they won through without serious loss. Harry was clearly rattled by the whole experience at Fort Cox. In a mood of furious anger, he demanded that the settlers 'rise up and destroy the barbarous savages', and drive out the Gaikas forever.

This emotional outburst was to cost Harry dear. When the words that he had spoken in fury after the crisis in Fort Cox reached Cape Town, most sections of opinion were horrified. Worse, they were reported to Whitehall, and Grey sent a severe rebuke, pointing out in a condescending and supercilious way that Harry's responsibility was not to exterminate but to civilize these fierce barbarians. Fortunately for

Harry, the Duke of Wellington, who was to support him once again and not for the last time, had been involved with Grey in discussions about troop reinforcements and had proposed the immediate dispatch of the Highland Light Infantry to help solve the security problems on the frontier. Meanwhile Harry was fully stretched, organizing the defence of a string of forts from Fort Cox down to the coast at East London against a widespread uprising. New difficulties quickly arose. The Hottentots, who had previously supported him, now rose in revolt under leaders, some of whom had been trained in the CMR, and were more dangerous foes. Harry, severely rattled and with his former confidence now undermined, felt that his tough approach had failed, so he treated the Hottentot rebels leniently, which enraged the frontier Boers. He also held a parade of those left in the CMR, flanked by two British units, told the Regiment that they were disgraced and made them lay down their arms. He allowed white members to keep their weapons, thus adding to the division between black and white, which was already at a dangerous level. All these difficulties were now compounded by the refusal of both Boer and British settlers to volunteer for security operations because in such a volatile situation they would not leave their homes and families unprotected. Feelings of insecurity grew daily, and hundreds of settlers flocked for safety into Port Elizabeth and Grahamstown.

Contemporary accounts paint a vivid picture of a deeply divided, bitter and apprehensive society. Somerset, one of the field commanders, had been promoted through the 'system', although Harry suspected he was incompetent – others described him as totally useless and altogether corrupt. Different groups came to Harry with ideas for their own protection, but, apart from swearing colourful oaths, he could do little to help them until reinforcements arrived. The grave situation on the frontier caused officials back in Cape Town to recruit many undesirables, who accepted the bounty of £25 but who proved troublesome, insubordinate and useless as soldiers. In his acute dilemma, Harry even thought of appealing to the Zulus, who might have welcomed the chance to strike at their traditional enemies, the Hottentots, but Shepstone (later Sir Theo Shepstone), a widely respected figure in Natal, managed to dissuade him from such a disastrous course. In spite of all the difficulties, by the end of March

1851, over 8,000 troops of varying quality had assembled on the frontier. With the settlers expecting Harry to mete out dire punishment to the rebels, here again the loss of his previous confidence became apparent. Initially, he sent out fairly strong patrols, but there were few good leaders and little was achieved. He was not well served by his subordinates. Somerset again proved his incompetence and Mackinnon was nicknamed 'Regulate the Pace' by the soldiers for his timidity.

Although Harry was still far from fit, it seems that the challenge, danger and excitement of his situation did restore his vigour and energy. A young officer noted his active and commanding presence. It therefore fell to Harry, now over sixty years old, to lead the assembled forces: some 2,000 infantry, mostly regular units bolstered by some recently enlisted riff-raff, some 9-pounders and a scratch group of mounted men. They faced formidable opposition. The Gaikas had learnt much, and from their strongholds in the hills to the east and north of Fort Cox they conducted an effective type of guerrilla war, led by the able and embittered Macomo. Faced by these problems, Harry complained that he was not receiving the support from the Boer farmers that he had done in 1835. Towards the end of March 1851, a fairly large group of Gaika warriors was located in the hills to the east of Fort Cox. Harry, now in his element, sent forward fighting patrols, cut off the enemy's retreat and inflicted a serious defeat. To teach them a salutary lesson he burnt down their villages. The Highlanders took the lead in attacking enemy units and effectively dispersed Macomo's main force. Local papers, both on the frontier and in Cape Town praised Harry's conduct of the operations. The *Cape Town Mail* reported: 'All speak of the bravery and activity of His Excellency.'

Harry had been reinvigorated by the challenge of the frontier, but back in Cape Town Juana was still depressed by the abrupt change from warm affection to outright hostility shown to them during the convict crisis, and now again worried about her Enrique and the adverse reports from the frontier. News that filtered back often stressed the setbacks and failures, and the growing strength of the rebels. It was even discovered that some mail had been intercepted and taken to Uithaalder, the ex-CMR leader of the Hottentot rebels. Thereafter Harry and Juana corresponded in Spanish. Juana, of course, knew the frontier and with her experience of years of campaigning took an intense interest in every detail of the operations, occasionally even making suggestions about the campaign. She had been encouraged when the Highland Light Infantry arrived, but was infuriated by the demanding attitude of some of the officers' wives. During May and June 1851, although substantial supplies and reinforcements arrived on the frontier, the military position hardly improved. Juana realized that Harry was doing his best to cover up bad news and consequently worried even more.

The lack of real success for the British units meant that some chiefs and some tribes were wavering in their loyalty. In view of this, at the end of June 1851, when the Highlanders had reached the frontier, Harry organized a strong four-pronged attack on Macomo's base in the Amatola Hills. This led to some fierce clashes, the destruction of a number of kraals and the capture of hundreds of cattle, but it did not defeat Macomo, who withdrew with his forces into the hills, ready to fight another day. Harry had to admit, in a dispatch to Grey, that such successes did little to bring the war to an end. He had been encouraged by a personal letter from Wellington, supporting his policy, but he was aware of the increasing criticism in Parliament about the continuing and growing expense of the war, which the Opposition had predicted.

Just when slightly better news came from the Amatolas, Harry's deputy, Major Warden, reported a dangerous development from further east. There were fresh defections among the Hottentots in the Cape Corps and in the Orange River Sovereignty, with many of the Boers there refusing to assist him against Moshesh, while their fellow-countrymen over the Vaal were prepared to back them in their hostility to the British Government. Warden was therefore ordered to act only on the defensive until troops could be sent to him.

Harry, writing at the time to his sister Alice, gave vent to his bitterness and illustrated the stress he was under. He spoke of the Hottentots upon whom he had lavished favours, but who were now rebelling, as 'cruel, treacherous, ungrateful savages, ungrateful wretches'. He partly blamed the Hottentot uprising on the missionaries who 'stirred them up'. In addition to these immediate problems, he had to suffer from ill-informed and malicious criticism in the House of Commons, 'which was ludicrous', and to which he could not respond. In another letter, one of Harry's nephews who was with him, also described the Hottentot attacks on defenceless farmers. He stressed the need for two or three more regiments, 'For without them, to end the war with his present force is impossible.'

While these troubles continued, two Commissioners, a Major Hogge and his assistant came out to the frontier. Ostensibly, they came to assess the seriousness of the unrest, but in fact had come in order to report directly to Grey, who had begun to have doubts about Harry's role and his policy. The Commissioners focussed on whether, in view of the tribal unrest and the strong opposition of the Boers, the Orange River Sovereignty should be abandoned. When this was discussed, Harry assured Grey that the rebels would see it as a victory and it would be a signal for revolt across the whole territory. From this time onwards, the main issues were decided not on the ground on the frontier, but by pressures in Whitehall, in Parliament and in Cape Town. While problems mounted, the Commissioners interviewed Pretorius, still the leader of the Voortrekkers, and in the Sand River Convention of 1852 agreed to the independence of the Boer territory north of the Vaal River – the Transvaal. Harry felt his powers being whittled away, and became increasingly embittered by the mounting criticism from Cape Town, from London and by Grey's growing disapproval. Grey, who never really understood the actual situation in the Cape, did at last realize that the war could not be won with the forces currently in the territory. He therefore ordered that two further regiments – the 12th Lancers and the 60th Rifles – were urgently dispatched.

An uneasy lull continued for several months, but was suddenly broken in September 1851, when Macomo, who had been building up supplies of weapons and ammunition in his strongholds in the Amatola Hills, launched attacks across the frontier area, destroying farms and taking away hundreds of cattle. Some more British reinforcements had arrived, including the 2nd of Foot (later the Queen's Royal Regiment) and more Highlanders, but they were ill-prepared and ill-equipped for the new type of guerrilla warfare which was being waged against them. In early skirmishes the Highlanders had twenty casualties and the Queen's nearly fifty. In the face of such serious reverses, the settlers, as well as the local papers on the frontier and in Cape Town, began to mount strong attacks on Harry. They blamed him for his utter conceit, for loss of military judgement and now for being despised by the Kaffirs. Some critics did make allowance for his age and for his recent illness, but few supported him.

Faced by growing and intractable problems, there is little doubt that, in order to impress Grey, Harry made many exaggerated claims about successes in the field. He still failed to realize that the two Commissioners, and particularly the senior one, Major Hogge, with their direct access to Grey, were seriously undermining his position. Their largely negative reports contrasted starkly with his claims of outstanding successes. Military failures continued through October and November, even though, with the arrival of the Suffolk Regiment from Mauritius and the 12th Lancers, Harry had over 6,000 troops under his command. In December 1851, despite concern about his health, he led a strong force over the Kei River, captured thousands of cattle and forced most of the chiefs to sue for peace. Here Harry's judgement was once again called in question. Macomo, whose antagonism had stemmed from his humiliation by Harry, swore he would rather die than be humiliated again. Harry remained obdurate and was determined that some of the rebel leaders should be hanged. Tense negotiations failed and he came under increasing pressure from Grey, who had received alarming reports from Hogge about supplies of arms to the rebels. Grey, too, was under pressure from the Opposition in Parliament over the escalating cost of the war and his dispatches became increasingly petulant, because he no longer believed Harry's claim of successes on the frontier.

The future of Harry and Juana was decided, not on the Kei River or in Fort Cox, but in a series of crisis meetings in London during December 1851. Grey had finally lost confidence in Harry and discussed the matter with Lord Russell, the Prime Minister. Their main problem was Wellington, who still supported Harry, and argued that the widespread war of colour was not Harry's fault. Then in January 1852, having managed to convince Queen Victoria, Grey sent the dispatch which dismissed Harry:

We have been compelled to believe that, perhaps from the failure of your health, and your being no longer able to exercise as close a personal superintendence as formerly over the conduct of affairs, you have failed in giving either to your military operations or to your political measures bearing upon the war, that character of vigour and judgment which are necessary to inspire confidence in the inhabitants and troops, and to command success.

It took weeks to arrive. Harry, still on the frontier in March 1852, was leading a spirited attack, accompanied by the usual bloodthirsty threats and oaths, when he received Grey's dispatch of January, with its shattering news. His dismissal caused furious discussion at the highest level in London, where Wellington and many others considered that Harry had been treated shamefully. Early in February, Wellington spoke in the House of Lords, saying he approved of all Harry had done, concluding his speech with: 'I have not observed any serious error in the conduct of the whole of these operations of my gallant friend Sir Harry Smith.' In the House of Commons there was even fiercer criticism of Grey when the whole episode was called a dirty business and he was charged with blackening Harry's character. Outside the House, critics reviled Grey for his arrogant insolence and a wave of sympathy supported Harry. He could not have known it at the time, but before he received his dismissal in the middle of March 1852, the crisis over the Cape had been a factor in bringing down Russell's government on 27 February, and Grey himself had been dismissed.

At one stage it looked as if General Cathcart, who had been appointed to succeed Harry, would travel on the ship which brought Grey's dispatch, but fortunately this was avoided. However, he did arrive soon afterwards, on 21 March, when Harry was still on the frontier, and Juana had the unenviable task of looking after him. He spent only a few days before setting off for the frontier and on 10 April he met Harry in King William's Town, where the handover took place. For the remainder of their stay in the Cape, Harry and Juana suffered a prolonged emotional storm. After handing over to Cathcart, which he did with courtesy and dignity, Harry left for East London, escorted by the local chiefs and their warriors. At the port he was so overcome with emotion and was so unwell that he had to be helped aboard the unfortunately named ship, *Styx*.

The ship reached Cape Town on 14 April 1852 and, rather to his surprise, Harry received a cordial and enthusiastic welcome. Thousands had gathered at the port and all the ships in the harbour hoisted their colours. He made a very short speech and then went at once to the Castle where Juana greeted him. In the short time since news of Harry's dismissal had arrived, Juana had the melancholy task of selling most of their possessions and handing over their home to their successor – a dismal experience, well known to Service families the world over. In spite of the violent criticism Harry and Juana had received during the convict crisis, opinion in Cape Town was now almost united in feeling that their treatment by Grey was savage, mean and shabby. In the days after his return, streams of visitors came to pay their respects, but Juana had to deal with these because Harry was confined to bed. He was too ill to attend a public dinner in his honour, although he did issue a statement with restrained and dignified comments:

> In the service of this colony I have spent some of the best years of my life, and, excepting those during which I have been Governor, some of the happiest. At such a moment as this, nothing can be remembered by me, and I am equally certain nothing can be remembered by the citizens of Cape Town and the colonists at large, excepting what would serve to keep alive old kindness and good feeling, and to bury all past differences and temporary estrangements in oblivion.

To the tradesmen and mechanics who came to see him off he said, 'I am myself a working man. Whatever reputation I may have at any time possessed, I gained simply and solely by being a working man who put his heart into his work.'

Then, only three days after his return, he and Juana were taken in a carriage, pulled by loyal citizens, from their home to the port. Harry, looking drawn and pale, did his best to acknowledge the cheers, while Juana sat beside him weeping. As they boarded the *Gladiator* for their journey back to Portsmouth, his staff thought that he seemed so ill he would not survive the voyage. Juana was overcome and wept bitterly. The ship left at 6.00am on 18 April 1852.

## Chapter 10

# Final Years
# June 1852 to October 1872

W hen Harry embarked at Cape Town he had been alarmingly sick and exhausted, and Juana had been very close to a breakdown. The six-week-long, uneventful voyage did much to restore them both, but the nature of Harry's dismissal and the anguish it caused them was never far from their minds. There was no escaping the fact that Harry was coming back under a cloud. In the eyes of the Whigs, he had not made a success of his Governorship. However, before they reached England, Lord Russell's government had fallen and Earl Grey with it. Harry's supporters, amongst whom there were still many who had never forgotten the hero of Aliwal, were quick to label Harry as the unfortunate scapegoat who had taken the blame for Grey's inadequate administration of the Colonies. Harry had had significant problems – the convict question, the Representative Assembly, lack of sufficient seasoned troops, difficulties with the Boers and local levies – that were either simply not understood in Whitehall or ignored. The eighth Frontier War of 1850-1853 was, arguably, the most critical armed emergency in South Africa to the present day. Some will dispute that and cite the Boer War of 1899-1902 but, judged in the context of its time, the threat to the survival of white civilization in 1851 was more serious than any since. Sarcastic letters from Grey, a civilian half Harry's age, were unhelpful. Some went as far as to say Harry's treatment had hastened the Government's collapse. True or not, it probably made him even more popular.

To Harry's great credit, he made little of this and with characteristic equanimity he and Juana were determined to settle down after many years abroad. Juana had long since severed all ties with Spain, her family had dispersed or had died and she had nothing to go back for. Her life, as it had been since she was fourteen, was with her beloved Enrique. Harry was now sixty-five which, by most standards, even of today, was an age to consider retirement – not him though. The arid desert of retirement, divorced from his beloved soldiery, was something that he just simply could not contemplate. Charlie Beckwith echoed these feelings to him in a letter: 'We should all die in our boots, with our spurs on, if possible; at any rate, the grand affair is to keep the game alive to the last.' Harry's sentiments exactly, no doubt reinforced by Juana, who realized that retirement would be the worst possible option for him. Harry most certainly intended to 'keep the game alive'.

The day after their arrival at Portsmouth on 1 June, Harry and Juana were formally addressed by the Mayor and Corporation of the town, who expressed their admiration for Harry's 'capacity and fitness for command in unparalleled difficulties'. Whether the Corporation was in a position to make such a judgement is neither here nor there; the point was that they were demonstrating their strong disapproval of Grey's judgement. Harry explained that he had been appointed 'Governor without a Legislative Council and a Commander-in-Chief without a British Army'. The *Portsmouth Times* of 5 June 1852 reported that his speech at a subsequent public meeting of the inhabitants showed his magnanimous spirit towards the Government that had, effectively, sacked him. Indeed, this was very much his attitude thereafter. Despite the temptation to make much of his own case and criticize the now fallen Government, he displayed a generous and good-natured approach to politicians, particularly Grey, who, he felt, were only doing their duty. Later he wrote:

> All England upon my arrival again received me with open arms. I was requested to stand as a member for Cambridge, for Westminster, for Edinburgh, for Glasgow. I declined to interfere with politics or to embarrass Her Majesty's Government, which I say my position enabled me to do, had not my desire been ever to serve it faithfully and fearlessly.

After arrival in London, he was determined to follow this line to the extent of accepting an invitation to dine with Grey. The latter was particularly grateful for this generosity of spirit and wrote:

> On a question of this kind we were not at liberty to consult our private feelings. This was fully understood by Sir Harry Smith himself, of whose most handsome and honourable conduct I cannot too strongly express my sense. He has shown no resentment against us for what we did, but has fairly given us credit for having been guided only by considerations of public duty. I feel individually very deeply indebted to him for the kindness with which he has acted towards me since his return.

Whatever criticisms were rightly levelled at Harry, lack of gentlemanly behaviour and good manners were not among them.

However, the invitation he really did appreciate was the one to a banquet from his beloved Duke to dine at Apsley House on 18 June to celebrate the Battle of Waterloo. This turned out to be the last ever held. Together with the Duke were Prince Albert, the Duke of Cambridge and thirty or forty generals who had distinguished themselves during the Napoleonic Wars. To his immense pleasure, the assembled company enthusiastically drank Harry's health, and recollections and reminiscences flowed amongst the old soldiers.

Juana and Harry settled comfortably near Havant in Hampshire and eagerly awaited notification of Harry's next appointment, which Harry was sure was imminent. In the meantime, he was invited over to Guernsey where his old friend, Sir John Bell, as Lieutenant Governor, persuaded Harry to address the local Guernsey militia. Harry was a great supporter of what we would now call the Territorial Army, having started his career in their ranks. He warmed to a favourite theme of the need, and ability, of locally recruited levies to defend their homeland. In a rousing speech he said:

> In the mountains of the Tyrol, under Hofer, the militia peasantry of the country repelled the attacks of the well-trained battalions of Napoleon. In Algeria for nearly thirty years have the peasantry defended their country, which even now is not conquered,

although 450,000 French soldiers have been sent there. In the
Caucasian Mountains the peasantry have resisted for thirty years
the efforts of 800,000 Russian soldiers to subjugate them, and the
Russians have made to this hour no progress. In South Africa I
have experienced what the determined efforts of an armed
peasantry can do, for after having beaten the Kaffirs in one place,
they immediately appeared in another. I state this to you to show
what a brave and loyal people as you are, are capable of doing.

While they might not have relished being addressed as 'peasantry', they
certainly would have been impressed at having this wartime hero in their
midst.

To Harry's great distress, he learned, when dining with the well-
known Napier brothers, Charles and William, that the Duke of
Wellington had died on 14 September. Harry had lost not only his
mentor and idol, but also a genuine friend and active supporter.
Wellington was buried at St Paul's Cathedral with a State Funeral
attended by a million and a half people. Harry rode in the procession as
a standard bearer, his final tribute to an adored leader.

In January 1853, Harry was at last appointed to command Western
District and to be Lieutenant Governor of Plymouth. With great
enthusiasm, Juana and he set up house in Devonport and dispensed
hospitality with characteristic generosity. The year 1854 saw the full
gloomy impact of the Crimean War and troops were constantly being
drafted from his Command and embarked through Plymouth, so he saw
much of them. The frustration of not being on active service must have
irked him, but he spent much time visiting and encouraging his units.
Raw troops, anxious about their first taste of active service, would have
been much impressed and heartened by this highly experienced veteran.
Harry was still able to ride his beloved horse, Aliwal (see plate section,
photo 15) and on an inspection they would charge the line of infantry he
was reviewing, but pull up abruptly just short of the front rank in a
flurry of hooves. This alarming trick must have initially surprised the
soldiery, but the word soon got round that this odd little general behaved
in this way. They were prepared for it and stood fast. Both Juana and
Harry were immensely popular in local society where, from time to time,

Harry would wear his Rifle green uniform, cutting a slightly quixotic figure with his small and spare build.

Characteristically, in the Rifle Brigade way, Harry never forgot an old soldier. There was a comradeship between officers and men in the 95th that was not widespread in the rest of the Army at the time. Johnny Kincaid, probably Harry's oldest friend, called the 1st Battalion the 'band of brothers'. Charlie Beckwith wrote to George Simmons, another survivor of the wars forty years before: 'Our friends it is true are fast descending into the tomb and we shall soon follow; but we shall lay down by the side of brothers who loved us during our lives. [They] and a long list down to the rank and file were all united in one common bond of common danger and suffering. God bless them all!' Here is Harry writing to an old soldier, Sergeant Himbury:

Government House, Devonport, May 20th, 1853.

OLD COMRADE HIMBURY,

I well recollect you. Upon the receipt of your letter of the 16th inst., I recommend your memorial to 'The Lords and other Commissioners of Chelsea Hospital' to have your pension increased to two shillings a day. There are few men now remaining in the British Army who have seen so much service and been in so many actions as yourself; and the fact alone, of your having been wounded when one of the Forlorn Hope at the important storm of San Sebastian, where we, the Light, Third, and Fourth Divisions sent our gallant volunteers, is enough. The Lords Commissioners are very kind to such gallant old soldiers as yourself, and, if they can increase your pension, I am sure they will. Let this certificate accompany your memorial, and let me hear that another, though not a forlorn, hope has succeeded. My wife well remembers your picking her up when her horse fell upon her, and again thanks you.

Your old friend and comrade,
H.G. SMITH, Major-General,
Colonel 2nd Battn. Rifle Brigade.

What Harry and his fellow officers understood was that men fight well when they are among their friends. Nebulous thoughts of fighting for the Country or their Division were too distant for many. What mattered to them was supporting the men about them and not letting them down. Their Platoon, Company and Regiment was what really mattered.

Harry, however, still champed at the bit and saw no reason why he should not be given a command in the Crimea. After all, he suggested, he was the same age as Raglan and there were others like Cathcart, who had relieved him in South Africa, who were not much younger. (Cathcart was subsequently killed at Inkerman.) Anyway, it was not to be and, of course, he had now also lost Wellington, his main supporter. This did not stop him, however, from writing to the new Commander-in-Chief, Lord Hardinge, whom he had well respected in the Punjab, to push cases of officers whom he had recommended for promotion for service in South Africa but had somehow missed out. By doing so, of course, he sought to keep his own name not far away from the Military Secretary's in-tray. To his pleasure, at least, Harry now became a substantive Lieutenant General (he had only held local rank in the Cape) and on 29 September 1854 was appointed Commander Northern and Midland Military District. Not the Crimea perhaps but, nevertheless, an important Home command. So Juana and he left Devonport for Manchester where they were to live until 1857. One of his first and most enjoyable duties was to arrange a reception for Queen Victoria in Hull on her journey south from Scotland. He was one of her most devoted servants, like many of his generation and there was nothing he would not do for her. On another occasion, he was honoured to represent the British Army at the funeral of Marshal St Arnaud, who had died in the Crimea, at Les Invalides in Paris. Harry had an audience with the Emperor who told him,

> You will see the Queen, and I pray you to assure Her Majesty how sensible I, the French Army and Nation are of the mark of respect paid to us by sending to attend the melancholy funeral of Marshal St. Arnaud, an officer of your rank and reputation with a Deputation of British Officers. The amicable relationship which existed between the Marshal and Lord Raglan renders his loss still more to be deplored.

Harry was now sixty-seven and, sadly, his friends were dying about him. His third 'Waterloo' brother, Charles, died on Christmas Eve 1854, followed shortly by Sir James Kempt, aged ninety. Sir Andrew Barnard's death came soon afterwards. Charlie Beckwith, a man of unusually mystical attitude who had devoted himself to an impoverished community in Piedmont, Italy, wrote to Harry:

> What a good old fellow Sir James was! I did not feel Sir Andrew's loss so much, as they told me that his intellect had failed. I had a good letter the other day from Lord Seaton. All these men I regard as the patriarchs of all that is solid in England. These men and their fellows, the men of Alma, Balaklava, Inkerman, of the *Birkenhead*, and the Arctic Regions, I hold to be the foundation-stones of England. In them is incarnate the sense of duty and obedience as a fixed habit, not a sentiment or conviction, as the people say, but a true witness of the Omnipotent who wills it thus ... Adieu. Love to Juana. We must expect to be rather rickety at the best, but we may toddle on. It is highly desirable that we may all go together as nearly as may be ... take care of your old bones, remember me kindly to any old fellow that may write to you, and believe me,

> Your affectionate friend,
> CHARLES BECKWITH

Juana was still the effervescent and outgoing character she had ever been. She wrote approvingly of Harry's adherence to the new regulation ordering officers to leave their upper lip unshaven: 'His marvellous moustaches are growing very nicely, and I do think they become his dear old face' (see plate section, photo 22).

On 29 June, the Queen visited the Art Treasures exhibition in Manchester, which had been opened by Prince Albert. As District Commander, Harry was responsible for military and security arrangements and, in procession, properly rode at the right rear wheel of the Queen's carriage, a position of importance in Palace protocol. When the Queen was about to knight the Mayor, she turned to Harry and, asking for his sword, told the Mayor, 'It has been in four general actions.'

On receiving it back, Harry pressed the hilt to his lips in salute to his monarch. Clearly impressed, the Queen said, 'Do you value it very much, Sir Harry?' Overcome, he presented it to her at once. Indeed he did value it – he had worn it since 1835 and it had been shot out of his hand at the Battle of Maharajpore. (Hanging beneath Harry's memorial in St Mary's Church, Whittlesey (see plate section, photo 20) is a sword, handed down through friends of Harry's in the town (see plate section, photo 18). The hilt/basket of the sword is actually damaged (see plate section, photo 19). Could this be the one he had shot out of his hand at the Battle of Marajpore and which he subsequently presented to Queen Victoria? Highly speculative and very unlikely, since, in a letter to the Lambert family from the Keeper of the King's Armoury, dated 5 July 1918, that sword, at the time of writing, was still in possession of the Royal Family.)

The summer of 1857 brought further gloom in the shape of the Indian Mutiny. This added to the worry and anxiety of people like Harry who had known the country and its soldiers so well. He had loved his Sepoys in the 1st Infantry Division who had fought so successfully in the Sikh Wars, and now this – he must have been in despair. That inveterate letter writer, Charlie Beckwith, continued to keep in touch with Harry, whom he admired as someone who he thought really knew what was going on in the world, whereas he confessed to relying on his own theories and the newspapers which he called 'two fallacious guides'. However, he never forgot to send his fondest love to Juana.

In May, Harry was back at the forefront of international affairs again. This time he was part of the delegation to Lisbon to invest Don Pedro V with the Order of the Garter on the occasion of his marriage to Princess Stephanie of Hohenzollern. Both Harry and Juana attended a Dinner and State Ball at Buckingham Palace to meet the Princess on her way to Portugal. In Lisbon, the King invested Harry with the Grand Cross of the Order of St Bento d'Aviz, which now hangs with Harry's other Orders and Decorations in possession of his great-great-nephew (see plate section, photo 25). What thoughts must have gone through Harry's mind when he recalled his convalescence there, forty-eight years before, when he was recovering from the wounds he received on the Coa.

Sadly, on his return, he was told his other great friend, George Simmons, who had also convalesced with him, had died.

On 9 October 1858, Harry inspected, for what was to be the last time, the 1st Battalion of the Rifle Brigade. He had them drawn up into a square and told them of his lifelong affection for the Regiment, what outstanding soldiers they were and, no doubt, a few soldier-like anecdotes, without deleting the expletives. There can have been few dry eyes on his departure.

Early the following year, Harry fell badly, cutting his knee. This was serious at his age – medicine being what it was in those days – and, understandably, caused Juana considerable anxiety. Beckwith, typically, made light of it and told him: 'he would have profited from this martyrdom which would fit him better to fall in with the ranks of the celestial army.' In fact, he very nearly lost his leg. The irony was not lost on him – it was the one the surgeons nearly removed after the Coa.

In September 1859, Harry's five-year posting in Manchester came to an end and, despite pleading with the Duke of Cambridge for a further appointment, he finally retired. There were many friends who wrote farewell letters to him and he, of course, replied with his customary punctiliousness. But there was one parting which was the saddest of all – from his beloved horse, Aliwal, now twenty-two. Harry had ridden him at Maharajpore and all the Sutlej battles; he had been transported to England, then to South Africa and back again. A sad account comes from the daughter of Harry's ADC, Major Payne:

> My sister and I have a vivid recollection of the lovely horse, and how, when we used to meet Sir Harry when we were out walking and he was riding, he would call out, 'Stand still, children,' and then come galloping up at full speed, and Aliwal would stop at our very feet; and my mother used to tell us that on the anniversary of the Battle of Aliwal, when there was always a full-dress dinner at the General's house, some one would propose Aliwal's health, and Sir Harry would order him to be sent for. The groom would lead the beautiful creature all round the dinner-table, glittering with plate, lights, uniforms, and brilliant dresses, and he would be quite quiet, only giving a snort now and then, though, when his health

had been drunk and the groom had led him out, you could hear him on the gravel outside, prancing and capering. The horse was now old, and Sir Harry, in his new house in London, would not be able to keep him; and though Sir Robert Gerard (now Lord Gerard) kindly offered him a home, Sir Harry feared that his old age would perhaps be an unhappy one, and he resolved to shoot him. My father and the faithful groom were with Sir Harry when he did so, and I believe they all shed tears.

On leaving Manchester, Harry and Juana took up residence in London. Harry was not, however, prepared to accept the quiet life. He immersed himself in Home Defence matters, wrote letters to *The Times* and exchanged forthright views with anyone who was prepared to listen. Even in February 1860, he was encouraging his old friends in Glasgow to establish a call-up system for home defence volunteers. Despite being seventy-two years old, he wrote: 'Should any enemy have the audacity to attempt our shores, could he avoid our ever invincible Navy, I as a General of some experience in war, would be proud to command a combined force.' In his heart of hearts, he knew this was not to be so. He disliked London and hated eking out an existence, counting his pennies. He worried about Juana when he had gone and wanted to ensure she had a pension appropriate to his rank. On 12 October 1860, his courageous old heart gave out. He was aged seventy-three.

Harry wanted to be interred at St Mary's, Whittlesey, but it was now closed to further burials. However, his body was taken there and in a corner of the new cemetery he was laid to rest on 19 October. All business in the little town was suspended for the day, and some thousands of the inhabitants and those of the outlying district lined the route of the procession. The Rifle Corps of Ely, Wisbech, March, Ramsey and Whittlesey were represented at their own request, and with arms reversed preceded the hearse from the station to St Mary's Church, and then to the cemetery. The coffin was borne by eight old soldiers who had all served under Harry and all wore their medals; the pall-bearers were six Whittlesey men, most of them his schoolfellows. Among the mourners were his surviving 'Waterloo brother', Tom, his nephew Hugh, Colonel Garvock, his Military Secretary in the Cape, and senior military officers. Three volleys were fired over the grave by the Volunteers. Over £700 was subscribed to found a memorial to his memory, and was spent on the restoration of the chapel at the end of the south aisle of St Mary's Church, where he had received his early education when it was used as a schoolroom. It is now known as 'Sir Harry's Chapel'. On the south wall was erected a monument of white marble surmounted by a bust of Sir Harry (see plate section, photo 20). It bears the inscription:

> This monument was erected and this chapel restored in 1862 by public subscription to the memory of Lieutenant-General Sir Harry G.W. Smith, Baronet of Aliwal, Knight Grand Cross of the Most Honourable Order of the Bath, Colonel of the 1st Battalion, Rifle Brigade. He entered the 95th Regiment in 1805, served in South America, Spain, Portugal, France, North America, the Netherlands, India, and at the Cape of Good Hope, of which he was Governor and Commander-in-Chief from 1847 to 1852, and on the Home Staff to 1859, when he completed a most gallant and eventful career of fifty-four years' constant employment. He was born at Whittlesey, 28th June, 1788 [sic – it was actually 1787], and died in London 12th October, 1860. Within these walls he received his earliest education, and in the cemetery of his native place his tomb bears ample record of the high estimation in which his military talents were held by his friend and chief, the great Duke of Wellington.

> Coruna, Busaco, Fuentes d'Onoro, Ciudad Rodrigo, Badajoz, Salamanca, Vitoria, Pyrenees, Nivelle, Nive, Orthez, Toulouse, Waterloo, Maharajpore, Ferozeshuhur, Aliwal, Sobraon, South Africa.

> O Lord, in Thee have I trusted; let me never be confounded.

After her husband's death, Juana lived in Hastings for a time, and then later at 79 Cadogan Place, London. Passionately cherishing her husband's memory, she was much loved by all the members of his family and their many friends. Finally, on 10 October 1872, she died aged seventy-four, and she was laid together with her beloved husband in his last resting place at Whittlesey (see plate section, photo 27).

Throughout their lives, Harry and Juana appeared to be hard up, and Harry always seemed to miss out on the lucrative rewards which could descend on successful commanders. He had been particularly incensed when Napier – far junior to him – received £50,000 for the capture of Sind. To his dying day, Harry's concern was for Juana, and he did all he could to ensure that if she outlived him, as was likely, she would be able to live in suitable style. Fortunately, both their wills have survived and they throw an interesting light on the true financial situation. Harry's will, signed on 30 July 1860, and full of the legal jargon of the day, left everything, 'all and singular, whatsoever and wheresoever', and including all his military medals, 'to my dear wife Juana'. Then, surprisingly, the next item is given to an Ellen Hermann – thought to be their housekeeper in Manchester – his gold watch and chain, together with twelve silver spoons and forks and a large gravy spoon. In addition, Ellen was to receive £500 if she outlived Juana. The will was witnessed by their old friend John Bell.

This gave little indication of the value of the estate, but Juana's will, made in October 1872, is full of more interesting detail – which proved that she had indeed been well provided for. Juana appointed as Executors, General Holdich, who had been Harry's ADC, and her nephew, Captain Lambert. Her main bequest of £1,500 went to the wife of Captain Lambert, who also received 'my household linen and my Indian and other diamonds'. Juana, who had no direct relatives of her own, had always been warmly welcomed into the large Smith family in Whittlesey, and she had become a firm favourite to large numbers of nephews, nieces and godchildren. Her will includes £100 to her servant; £25 to each of five godchildren; £50 to her brother-in-law Tom; bequests of £50 or £25 to ten nephews and nieces, but 'not to Eleanor because she is well provided for'. Finally, she divided the residue of her estate between six named nephews and nieces.

Of the other close friends and companions of Harry's, Charlie Beckwith died in July 1862, among the Piedmontese whom he had served so devotedly, and Sir John Bell in 1876, having lived to the age of ninety-four. Of his family, Harry's sister, Jane Alice, later Mrs Sargant (of whom it has been said that she was 'the only person in the world of whom he was afraid') – to whom he wrote copious letters, particularly from South Africa and India, many of which are in the National Archives at Kew – died in 1869. His youngest sister, Anna Maria, died in 1875. His brother, Tom, born in 1792, was commissioned into the 95th in 1808, and took part in Sir John Moore's expeditions and the Battle of Corunna. Like Harry, he served with the Light Division throughout the Peninsula War up to the Battle of Toulouse, being badly wounded at the Coa. He was recommended for promotion for his conduct at Waterloo. He proceeded with his Regiment to Paris, and, riding as Adjutant at the head of the 2nd Battalion, was the first British officer to enter the city on 7 July 1815. On retirement he was made a Companion of the Order of the Bath and granted a special pension. He died in London on 6 April 1877 and was buried in the cemetery at Aldershot. His medals are currently in possession of his great-grandson. Another brother, Charles, born in 1795, fought as a Volunteer (he was actually too young to enlist properly) with the 1st Battalion of the 95th at Quatre Bras and Waterloo, after which he received a commission as Second Lieutenant. Two or three years later he retired from the Army and settled at Whittlesey. He was a stalwart of local society becoming a JP, Deputy Lord Lieutenant for Cambridgeshire and a Lieutenant Colonel in the Yeomanry, dying at Whittlesey on 24 December 1854. Tom's daughter, Annie, married Wellesley Robinson. They had a son, Annesley, who in turn had a son, Christopher, born in 1930, who, as Harry's great-great-nephew happily survives to this day.

So, what of the character of these two people? Harry was impetuous, headstrong and, without a doubt, courageous. So was Juana, which was extraordinary for a young girl of her sheltered and convent-educated background. They were both fiery tempered but resilient in adversity and able to put up with significant physical hardship. They leant on each other physically and emotionally to an unusual extent for their times.

Harry was also intolerant and arrogant, almost to the point of insolence – take, as examples of this, his treatment of General Lowry Cole in the Peninsula and his remarks to General Pakenham at New Orleans. He was self-opinionated and regarded his own views as virtually unarguable. His three memos during the First Afghan War would earn a present-day serving officer severe displeasure from his superiors. Nevertheless he was, above all, a charismatic leader. There are any number of instances where Harry led from the front in the battles we have described. He looked after his men in a way which was rare in those days. He realized that they needed serviceable kit and proper resupply, training and rest when exhausted. Men followed him because they respected this and knew that he would not ask of them something he was not prepared to do himself. He took risks, both for himself and for his men, which, by the criteria of our current army, would be unacceptable, but we must judge really devastating battles, such as New Orleans, Badajoz and Waterloo, by the standards of the day. Even so, Harry felt the losses most strongly and, personally, to a remarkable extent. Officers up to a very senior level physically led their men and the battles are littered with generals killed and wounded – Craufurd, Pakenham, Ross, Picton and the like. While Harry commanded various groups of men from time to time, and formally as a company commander, he never actually commanded a battalion or brigade before becoming a divisional commander in the First Sikh War. Today this would be impossible, yet Harry's success is self-evident. He had learnt his skills by hard exposure to warfare and from others, rather than through a standard ascent up the military promotion ladder. At the same time, he also proved himself a consummate staff officer. Then, as today, to be a front-line soldier and administrator are not always the happiest of combinations. He relished his job as Town Major of Cambrai after Waterloo and then did remarkably well during the yellow fever epidemic in Jamaica. Of course he was ambitious, but so were his colleagues. Why otherwise did officers volunteer for the Forlorn Hope and relish battle since, bluntly, casualties produced gaps for advancement.

As a General, he had many of the skills and attributes that are easily recognizable today. He despised the frontal and manpower-expensive assault beloved by the unimaginative Gough at Ferozeshah and Ross at Bladensberg, preferring the indirect approach and the diversionary attack. Aliwal, now a relatively forgotten battle, was, at the time, considered a masterpiece of what we would now call 'all-arms cooperation'. Harry deftly organized his infantry, cavalry and artillery to support each other at the right time and right place – a task which was beyond many of his contemporaries who merely saw battle as a hard full-frontal slog. He understood the importance of timing and the critical point at which to mobilize his reserve, despite the difficulty of communication.

His selection for the Governorship of the Cape can be easily understood, even by standards of today. Here was a triumphant General, idolized by the public (and media such as existed then), praised by no less than the Duke of Wellington and, above all, already heavily experienced in the South African scene. Not only that, he had written an assessment of the situation in the eastern Cape and how to deal with it, which was widely accepted. Whitehall and Cape Town could hardly have had a more suitable candidate. But his instinct and judgement, so successful as a soldier, failed him as a diplomat. His inability to deal with the machinations of political expediency, both within government at home and the tiresome local disputes, over, for instance, the convict question and parliamentary reform in the Cape, led, inexorably, to his recall. The eighth Frontier War of 1850-1853 was, arguably, the most critical armed emergency in South Africa to the present day. Some will dispute that and cite the Boer War of 1899-1902, but judged in the context of its time, the threat to the survival of white civilization in 1851 was more serious than any since. Harry's judgement failed him and he remained mistakenly optimistic and overconfident. His assessment of people was not always sound and, despite his temper and irascible nature, he tolerated inadequate subordinates like Somerset, whom he should have removed at an early stage. He was, inevitably, then made the sacrificial lamb for a failing government in its last-ditch attempt to save itself. Was it really Harry's fault or the selectors who put him there? There is an uncomfortable saying, still current in modern military parlance, that some officers are promoted to one level above their competence. Was this so with Harry? He was what we would call today a 'soldier's soldier', an officer who was outstanding with his men and a master of his particular battlefield, but who, when promoted to the 6th Floor of the Ministry of Defence, finds himself outflanked and outwitted by clever civil servants, financiers and wily self-serving politicians.

Writers have blamed Harry's drive and the perception of self-aggrandisement on his humble upbringing and lack of money, but there is little real evidence for this, as we have seen. Wellington himself was often short of money, and this is simply the way people lived in times of great uncertainty and appalling financial administration. As for Harry being 'plebeian', this is absolute nonsense. Of course, he was no aristocrat but, as a surgeon, his father was a pillar of local society and three of his sons deserved their Commissions as well as anyone. Foulmouthed and irascible? Maybe, but again, only a product of the time. 'Black Bob' Craufurd was idolized by his men and yet had to be personally rebuked for his profanity by Wellington.

As a loving husband, and with a love fully reciprocated by Juana, it would be difficult in those times to find better. We are lucky enough to have access to records of husbands, sons and fathers who wrote letters copiously when on active service, and Harry and Juana were no exceptions. They were lucky to have suffered little real separation (only America) even by today's standards and no complications with children. Had they had any it is conceivable that things might have turned out differently. Juana gave up everything for Harry: country, family and friends. But she was happy to do so. They were generous with their money when they had it and easily made friends across the social spectrum. They were both equally at ease with the rough soldiery as they were with the crowned heads of Europe. They entertained well but not over-lavishly and much enjoyed other people's company. So, not a complicated mixture, but a mixture nevertheless of courage, impetuosity, charm, not always the best of judges, but, above all, with a sense of humour and happiness in each other's company.

Thus ends this extraordinary and enduring love story between two, on the face of it, ill-matched people: the distraught fourteen-year-old Spanish aristocrat fleeing the carnage of Badajoz, and the 25-year-old, combat experienced, worldly wise, English officer. They both had their tempers and tantrums, but like many that do, quickly made up and fell into each other's arms. They attracted devotion from those who surrounded them, the classic example being Harry's orderly, West. Juana endeared herself to the hard-bitten Peninsula soldiery amongst whom she slept, wrapped in a blanket by her horse, and with the Sepoys at

Maharajpore, riding her elephant into battle. Harry properly concentrated on his job in hand but he always had Juana's welfare in mind the moment he had a chance. He fully realized the anxieties she had when she knew he was away fighting. Juana was much loved by Harry's family and it was a mark of their character that they took this Spanish girl in so readily and made her one of them.

Harry's last thoughts were for Juana, her welfare and his great desire that they should be buried together.

They were, and were never again divided.

# Appendix 1

# Harry's Ranks and Appointments

## Regimental Rank

Second Lieutenant . . . . . . . . . . . . . . . . . . . . . . . . . . . . . . . . . . .8 May 1805
Lieutenant . . . . . . . . . . . . . . . . . . . . . . . . . . . . . . . . . . .15 August 1805
Captain . . . . . . . . . . . . . . . . . . . . . . . . . . . . . . . .28 February 1812
Major, unattached . . . . . . . . . . . . . . . . . . . . . . . .29 December 1826
Lieutenant Colonel, unattached . . . . . . . . . . . . . . . . . . . . . .22 July 1830
Lieutenant Colonel, 3rd Foot . . . . . . . . . . . . . . . . . . . . .13 May 1842
Lieutenant Colonel, unattached . . . . . . . . . . . . . . . . . .25 August 1843
Colonel, 47th Foot . . . . . . . . . . . . . . . . . . . . . . . . . . . . . . .18 January 1847
Colonel, 2nd Battalion Rifle Brigade . . . . . . . . . . . . . . . . . . .16 April 1847
Colonel, 1st Battalion Rifle Brigade . . . . . . . . . . . . . . . . . .18 January 1855

## Army Rank

Major . . . . . . . . . . . . . . . . . . . . . . . . . . . . . . . . . . . . . . . . .29 September 1814
Lieutenant Colonel . . . . . . . . . . . . . . . . . . . . . . . . . . . . . . . . . . .18 June 1815
Colonel . . . . . . . . . . . . . . . . . . . . . . . . . . . . . . . . . . . . . . .10 January 1837
Local rank of Major General in the East Indies . . . . .21 August 1840
Major General . . . . . . . . . . . . . . . . . . . . . . . . . . . . . . . .9 November 1846
Local rank of Lieutenant General in South Africa . . . . . . . . . . .1847–52
Lieutenant General . . . . . . . . . . . . . . . . . . . . . . . . . . . . . . .20 June 1854

# Staff Appointments

## Peninsula War

Aide de Camp to Colonel T.S. Beckwith ................October 1810

Brigade Major, 2nd Brigade, Light Division ...............March 1811
under Major General Drummond,                              to end of war
Major General Vandeleur, Major General                    March 1814
Skerrett and Colonel Colborne successively


## Washington Expedition

Deputy Adjutant General to Major General R. Ross...............1814


## New Orleans Expedition

Assistant Adjutant General to Major General
Sir Edward Pakenham ...................................................1814
Military Secretary to Major General Sir James Lambert ..........1815


## Waterloo Campaign

Brigade Major, afterwards Assistant Quartermaster General
to 6th Division (Major General Sir James Lambert and
Major General Sir Lowry Cole successively)
[Returns to his regiment.]


## Occupation of France

Town Major of Cambrai .........................................1815–18
[Returns to his regiment.]

## Glasgow

Brigade Major to Major General Sir T. Reynell
(commanding Western District) and Lieutenant
General Sir Tom Bradford (Commander-in-Chief
in Scotland) successively.
[Returns to his regiment.] ........................................1819-25

## Nova Scotia

Aide de Camp to Lieutenant General
Sir James Kempt, Governor ...........................................1826

## Jamaica

Deputy Quartermaster General under
Lieutenant General Sir John Keane, Governor .....................1827

## Cape of Good Hope

Deputy Quartermaster General under Lieutenant General
Sir Lowry Cole, Lieutenant General Sir Benjamin D'Urban,
Major General Sir G.T. Napier, Governors, successively ......1828-1840
Chief of Staff under Sir Benjamin D'Urban
in the Kaffir War ........................................................1835

## India

Adjutant General to Her Majesty's Forces, under
Lieutenant General Sir Jasper Nicolls and Lieutenant
General Sir Hugh Gough, Commanders-in-Chief,
successively ...................................................1840-1845

## Sikh War

Commander 1st Division Infantry ................................1845-6

## Cape of Good Hope

Governor and Commander-in-Chief ...........................1847-52

## Home Staff

Commander Western Military District ..........................1853-4
Commander Northern and Midland Military Districts ..........1854-9

# Bibliography

Bunbury, Colonel T., *Reminiscences of a Veteran* (no publisher/date).
Fletcher, Ian, *Badajoz – Hell Before Daylight*, Baton Press, 1984.
——, *Badajoz 1812*, Osprey, 1999.
Fortescue, The Hon. J.W., *History of the British Army*, London, 1920.
Freemantle, A.F., 'Juana Maria de Los Dolores de Leon', *Army Quarterly*, vol. XXVI, 1933.
Glover, Michael, *Wellington's Army in the Peninsula 1808-1814*, David & Charles, 1977.
Harington, A.L., *Sir Harry Smith – Bungling Hero*, Tafelberg Publishers, 1980.
Heathcote, T.A., *The Afghan Wars 1839–1919*, Osprey, 1980.
Howarth, David, *A Near Run Thing*, Collins, 1968.
'Letter from Dr Brydon to his brother', *JSAHR*, vol. 51, No. 027, 1973.
'16th Lancers', *JSAHR*, vol. 61, in National Army Museum.
Kincaid, John, *Random Shots from a Rifleman*, 1835, in National Army Museum.
——, *Adventures in the Rifle Brigade*, Pen & Sword, 2005.
Lehmann, Joseph, *Remember You Are An Englishman*, Cape, 1977.
Liddell Hart, B.H. (ed), *The Letters of Private Wheeler*, Michael Joseph, 1951.
Longford, Elizabeth, *Wellington: The Years of the Sword*, Weidenfeld & Nicolson, 1969.
Lunt, James, *The Scarlet Lancers*, Leo Cooper, 1993.
Moore Smith, G.C. (ed.), *Autobiography of Lt Gen Sir Harry Smith*, London, 1903.
Morris, *Recollections of Sergeant Morris*, Windrush Press, 1998.

Napier, William, *History of the War in the Peninsula*, Elibron Classics, 2000.

Rooney David, *Guerrilla*, Brasseys, 2004.

Sale, Lady Florentia, *Journal of the Disasters in Afghanistan 1841-2*, Naval & Military Press, 2005.

Seymour, William, *History Today*, vol. 26, in National Army Museum.

South African Ladysmith Historical Society, *The Smiths of Ladysmith*, Blackwoods, 1939.

Unknown, *Regimental Nicknames and Traditions of the British Army*, Gale & Polden, 1915.

Urban, Mark, *Rifles*, Faber & Faber, 2003.

——, *The Man who Broke Napoleon's Codes*, Faber & Faber, 2001.

Windham, The Rt Hon. William, 'Orders to Maj Gen Craufurd', Downing Street, 30 October 1806.

# *Index*